"Carol Kent has long been one of my favorite authors because she can distill profound thoughts into a few words. *Becoming a Woman of Influence* is a fine example of her ability as she goes beyond telling us to follow Jesus' example to giving us specifics on how to do that. If you want to make a difference in today's world, this book is for you."

SANDRA P. ALDRICH,
speaker and author of *Bless Your Socks Off*

"There is a wealth of godly wisdom in Carol Kent's book, *Becoming a Woman of Influence*. The valuable, life-giving principles she shares are sure to renew your heart and move you closer to Christ."

CHERI FULLER,
speaker and author of *When Mothers Pray,
Quiet Whispers from God's Heart for Women*,
and other books

Making a Lasting Impact on Others

BECOMING A WOMAN *of* INFLUENCE

CAROL KENT

NAVPRESS®

BRINGING TRUTH TO LIFE

The Navigators is an international Christian organization. Our mission is to reach, disciple, and equip people to know Christ and to make Him known through successive generations. We envision multitudes of diverse people in the United States and every other nation who have a passionate love for Christ, live a lifestyle of sharing Christ's love, and multiply spiritual laborers among those without Christ.

NavPress is the publishing ministry of The Navigators. NavPress publications help believers learn biblical truth and apply what they learn to their lives and ministries. Our mission is to stimulate spiritual formation among our readers.

ISBN 1-57683-933-8

Cover design by The DesignWorks Group, www.thedesignworksgroup.com
Cover photo by iStock
Creative Team: Liz Heaney, Marla Kennedy, Lori Mitchell, Darla Hightower, Arvid Wallen, Pat Reinheimer

Some of the anecdotal illustrations in this book are true to life and are included with the permission of the persons involved. All other illustrations are composites of real situations, and any resemblance to people living or dead is coincidental.

Unless otherwise identified, all Scripture quotations in this publication are taken from *The Message: New Testament with Psalms and Proverbs* by Eugene H. Peterson, copyright © 1993, 1994, 1995, used by permission of NavPress Publishing Group. Other versions used include: the *HOLY BIBLE: NEW INTERNATIONAL VERSION* (NIV). Copyright © 1973, 1978, 1984 by International Bible Society, used by permission of Zondervan Publishing House. All rights reserved.

Kent, Carol, 1947-
    Becoming a woman of influence : making a lasting impact on others / Carol Kent.
       p.   cm.
    ISBN 1-57683-933-8 (pbk.)
    1. Christian women–Religious life. 2. Mentoring in church work. 3. Christian leadership. 4.
Kent, Carol, 1947-   I. Title.
BV4527.K448 1999
248.8'43 — dc21
                                           99-40979
                                       CIP

Printed in the United States of America

2 3 4 5 6 7 8 9 10 11 12 13 14 15 16 / 12 11 10 09 08 07 06

FOR A FREE CATALOG OF NAVPRESS BOOKS & BIBLE STUDIES,
CALL 1-800-366-7788 (USA) OR 1-800-839-4769 (CANADA)

This book is lovingly dedicated to my daughter-in-love,

April Dawn Kent

As an extraordinary woman of influence, you have
turned fear into faith,
faced a challenging future with courage,
nurtured and protected two beautiful little girls,
accepted all the transitions of a military wife,
lived without complaint on a shoestring budget, and
demonstrated the compassion and
unconditional love Jesus modeled.

I love you,
Mom

ACKNOWLEDGMENTS

This book is about people of influence — and I salute the individuals in my life who have made footsteps worth following. They made this book possible.

THE SPEAK UP SPEAKER SERVICES STAFF TEAM

My husband, Gene Kent: You keep me laughing, encouraged, and balanced. Partnering with you in ministry is such a personal and professional pleasure.

My administrative assistant, Laurie Dennis: You make every person who calls our office feel significant—what a gift! Your enthusiasm for this ministry, concern for our speakers, and efficient office skills are a rare combination. My cat likes you, too!

My office assistant, Shirley Liechty: Your care for details and your compassion for people have enriched our home office team. God knew we needed you!

FRIENDS WHO GAVE ME PERMISSION TO TELL THEIR STORIES IN THIS BOOK

A project like this could never have been as effective without the stories of real-life mentors and encouragers. Many of you filled out my lengthy survey and sent outstanding tributes and illustrations of how your life has been impacted by people of influence. I wish we could have included all of them.

I salute the following people who sent extraordinary contributions that appear in this book: Julie Baker, Jayne Clark, Sherrie Eldridge, Leola Floren, Cathy Gallagher, Judy Hampton, Deborah Henry, Bernadine Johnson, Meghan McIntosh, Barbara McPhail, Kim Moore, Pastor Jay Stewart, Martha Strickland, Nan Walker, Ruth Winslow, and Kathe Wunnenberg. Your stories put "heart and soul" into this project.

THE VALUED TEAM MEMBERS

The NavPress Publishing Group: You make me feel like a valued part of what God is doing through your publishing house. I feel supported, encouraged, and inspired by your enthusiastic response to my ideas. Thanks for being great cheerleaders!

Liz Heaney: You have a remarkable gift! Your ability to cut and paste turns ordinary chapters into works of art. Thank you for tenaciously holding a demand for excellence over my head until we got there. You are a woman of influence in my life!

The Intercessors: Every time I stand in front of an audience or write a chapter of a book, I know you are praying that God will do His supernatural work in the hearts of the listeners and the readers. Your prayers are the power behind the awesome things He is doing!

CONTENTS

How to Get the Most Out of This Book   11

One   Impacting Lives Like Jesus Did   13

Two   Learning from the Master   23

Three   The Principle of Time Alone with God   39

Four   The Principle of Walking and Talking   61

Five   The Principle of Storytelling   83

Six   The Principle of Asking Questions   101

Seven   The Principle of Compassion   117

Eight   The Principle of Unconditional Love   137

Nine   The Principle of Casting Vision   157

Nine-Week Bible Study   179

Notes   211

About the Author   217

How to Get the Most Out of This Book

I ALMOST CALLED THIS PAGE the *Foreword*, but I thought you might not read it if it had such a formal title. Since your time is so valuable, I want you to know from the first page how you will receive the greatest "impact value" from this book.

Researching and writing a book on influencing lives as Jesus did changed my approach to everyday life. I now view my daily interruptions, unexpected phone calls, and casual meetings with people as potential *impact moments — God appointments* that give me an opportunity to intentionally influence the lives of people who are in my path today.

There are two ways to read this book. If you are looking for inspiration, encouragement, and instruction on how to influence lives as Jesus did, you can begin with the first chapter and read straight through to the end of the book. However, if you would like the most value for your time and are willing to risk an adventure that could change your life, take a look at the Nine-Week Bible Study that begins on page 179 before you begin reading. It will give you step-by-step instructions for reading each chapter, memorizing appropriate Scripture, responding to Bible study questions, learning more about what Jesus taught about the principles discussed, and understanding how He modeled each one. It will also give you ideas for a "hands-on" approach to applying the principle you are studying.

The Bible study portion of this book can be used for individual or small group studies. Before you begin, ask God to make you tender to His truth and open to making definite changes in the way you respond to people. The influence this book talks about has nothing to do with selfish pride and with impressing people. It has everything to do with shaping your heart to the image of Jesus Christ and becoming a woman of influence who practices the principles He modeled. I hope you enjoy reading this book as much as I enjoyed writing it. If God uses this material to impact your life, I'd love to hear about it. Write me at: Speakupinc@aol.com.

Warmly,
Carol Kent

Chapter One

IMPACTING LIVES LIKE JESUS DID

Somewhere along the line every Christian woman wishes she had a sister to help her negotiate the twists and turns of life.[1]

— DONNA OTTO

I SAT IN THE AUDIENCE, moved by the unseen presence of Jesus Christ. As Corrie ten Boom spoke, the audience hung on every word. Some were taking notes. Many were wiping away tears. As I listened to her speak, I longed to connect with this Christlike woman who modeled "no strings attached" forgiveness and unconditional love. She had challenged and encouraged so many. How I wanted to impact lives as she did!

J. Oswald Sanders said, "Spirituality is not easy to define, but its presence or absence can easily be discerned. . . . It is the power to change the atmosphere by one's presence, the unconscious influence that makes Christ and spiritual things real to others."[2] That day Corrie ten Boom was the presence of Christ to me. Motivated by her example, I prayed that God would use me to inspire others to be like Christ. I wanted my life to count. I had a passionate desire to live a life that drew others to Jesus, but I wasn't sure how that desire would play out in my life.

ME? A WOMAN OF INFLUENCE?

During our first few years of marriage, my husband, Gene, and I were youth directors in a church in Newaygo, Michigan. During the day Gene taught English and journalism in a public school and I directed the

Alternative Education Program for Pregnant Teenagers. As director, I individualized curriculum so my students could stay in high school for the duration of their pregnancies. During my last year in the program I had sixty-eight pregnant, unwed students. Seven of them were only fourteen years old.

I soon discovered something surprising. Teenage girls were hanging out in my office before and after school, talking to me about makeup, boys, babies, life, God, and their relationship struggles at home. The same thing was happening before, during, and after youth events at church. I was being asked all sorts of questions by these teens:

- "I'm a new Christian and I have some questions about the Bible. Can you help me?"
- "I can't get along with my mother and dad. We fight all the time. How can we talk if we can't quit yelling?"
- "When you fell in love, how did you know Gene was the man you were supposed to marry?"
- "How can you know God's will for your life? I'm a senior and I have to decide what I'm going to do next year. My parents are putting pressure on me to apply to a college and I don't know what to do."
- "I have a friend who needs God in her life, but I'm shy about talking about my faith. What would you say to her if you were me?"

Even though I believed I needed to find an older, more mature Christian woman who could teach me how to mentor others, I began to realize I was already having an impact. These teenagers were looking to me for wise counsel and practical advice. I had never thought of myself as an "influencer," but it seemed natural to build relationships with these girls and to offer solid biblical answers to their questions. I was in a position to influence, whether I felt ready or not!

EACH OF US IS AN INFLUENCER

Recently a young woman told me about her eleventh-grade math teacher. It was near the end of the year and Meghan McIntyre was feeling isolated and hurt, searching for a reason to live. She said, "I was closer to choosing death than life." Then Meghan asked this teacher to sign her yearbook. Unaware of Meghan's emotional state, he wrote:

> *"Consider the lilies of the field. They sow not neither do they spin. Yet Solomon, in all his glory was not arrayed like one of these." If God so clothes the grass of the field, shall He not much more clothe you, Meghan? You have been a source of joy to me. Thanks for all your help in the math department, and may you achieve your goals with joy.*
> *Mr. Ottley*

Mr. Ottley's words, quickly jotted down in a high school yearbook, provided Meghan with warmth and with the hope that God might have something to offer her. She was incredulous that she had brought joy to someone else — or that someone might wish that *she* experience joy. Oh, how she wanted that very thing!

Mr. Ottley's words made Meghan curious — who was this God? Jesus commanded, "Go into all the world and preach the good news to all creation" (Mark 16:15, NIV). Mr. Ottley had taken the time to put in writing the good news that God cared for Meghan. His mission field included the school where he taught — and he proclaimed the good news to her, a student in his calculus class who needed hope. His words prepared the way for Meghan's life-changing encounter with Christ. In her first year of university, other Christians came and watered the seed Mr. Ottley had planted, and Meghan finally experienced new life in Jesus.

Mr. Ottley had no idea how his words had affected Meghan until his retirement party years later. As the floor was opened for comments, Meghan told her story, looked Mr. Ottley in the eyes, and said, "Thank you for writing in the yearbook of my life." This man had unintentionally influenced Meghan to search for the most important answers in life. He had simply lived as a Christian teacher should live and responded to her in a Christlike way.

We all influence people, whether we recognize it or not. However, it wasn't until I experienced a significant birthday that I determined to be more intentional about how I was influencing others.

SHAPING HEARTS INTO HIS IMAGE

My decision to be more intentional about how I influenced others was prompted by a personal milestone: another "decade marker" birthday. I had approached it with dread and apprehension, and I wanted this birthday to pass with little fanfare. However, my friends had other ideas.

On the evening of "the big day," Gene and I were invited to the home of friends. Upon arriving, we settled in for a night of great conversation. Suddenly there was a knock at the back door and in marched a room full of friends, many of whom I hadn't seen for a long time. Carrying black balloons and gag surprises, they sang "Happy Birthday," and the party began. Their gifts were insulting! Support hose, vitamins, fans for hot flashes, reading glasses, exercise videos, magazines for "retired folks," suggestions for menopausal madness, and laxatives. Lots of laxatives! We laughed, ate cake, remembered old times, and enjoyed the safety and security of relationships that had been forged over time.

The next day another gift arrived from a new friend, someone I had been mentoring by long distance. It was a book with these words inscribed inside the front cover: "Thank you for shaping my heart to His image." The words pierced my heart.

Over the next few months I received several notes from women with questions about God, parenting challenges, relationship struggles, job changes, and ministry choices. Many of these letters were from women who longed for a mentor. With each letter I became more certain that God wanted me to devote the last half of my life to influencing young leaders who would carry His work on to future generations.

I could think of no better model to follow than Jesus, so I began to study His life and how He related to people. The gospels tell us that Jesus poured His life into a few people, and in turn this small group impacted the world and all of history. We can't read Matthew, Mark, Luke, and John without coming across numerous examples of one-on-one encounters Jesus had with people — encounters that radically changed their lives.

One of my favorites is how Jesus interacted with Matthew, the tax-collector-turned-disciple. Jesus walked by Matthew's booth one day while he was on duty. There he was: a capable money handler, a leader, a man of authority and power . . . someone who might have skimmed some of the profits off the top. But Jesus saw Matthew with different eyes. He saw who Matthew could become — one of His biographers! He saw weaknesses that could be turned into strengths. He envisioned a transformed lifestyle. A new passion. A tenacious loyalty. As Jesus passed by, he called to Matthew, "Follow me." And Matthew did.

As I studied the life of Christ, I wanted to know more so that I could follow His example of how to influence people in ways that would make a lasting difference.

Once I had identified my purpose — studying how Jesus influenced lives, integrating those principles into my own life, and passing them on to the next generation — I experienced a freedom I hadn't felt for a long time. Always busy "doing," I often felt pulled in too many directions. I now had an outstanding reason to say, "No, I won't be able to accept that invitation because I am convinced God wants the concentration of my energy in another direction." It became easy to quickly and efficiently say yes to opportunities for ministry that were in line with my mission to evangelize, equip, encourage, and empower people to impact others with their God-given potential.

WHAT THIS BOOK IS AND WHAT IT IS NOT

Let me ask you a question: What would happen if you decided to influence lives on purpose? One of the reasons I'm writing this book is to challenge women to become more intentional about how we influence others, not because we *have* to, but because we *want* to. Not because it is our Christian obligation, but because it brings great meaning and joy to our lives. Not because of duty, but because of love. Let's be like Jesus.

Let's be women of conviction and passion. Let's intentionally influence other women because it is a high calling and a part of our predesigned purpose.

I didn't write this book to make women feel like failures as Christians if they have not made a lifetime commitment to mentor a younger woman, nor did I write it to present this model as the correct way to mentor. The sole purpose of this book is to inspire and equip women to impact lives as Jesus did.

Many of us have dreamed of having an older woman with whom we meet on a regular basis who will point out our gifts and provide advice, encouragement, and resources. Someone to give us wise counsel day or night, someone to whom we can speak our mind and tell our secrets, knowing they will be guarded carefully. Someone with whom to pray and dream. But sad to say, this "idealistic dream" is usually far from reality.

As part of my research for this book, I designed a survey that I sent to almost one hundred Christian leaders. One question asked whether the person had had a lifetime mentor. To my surprise, only a handful of these gifted Christian leaders had one mentor for life. Almost without exception, the respondents talked of many people who had influenced them in positive and life-changing ways. Sometimes this occurred through a one-time encounter; other times these mentors were influential for a period of time. A few of the individuals I surveyed said the person who had influenced them the most was a historical figure — obviously someone they had never even met!

Having said that, let's come full circle to the purpose of this book: learning to impact lives as Jesus did. As I've studied Christ's life, I've come up with seven principles for impacting the lives of the people around us in profoundly meaningful ways. Whether we act as lifetime mentors, friends, encouragers, or seasonal mentors, we can embrace and pass on the principles Jesus lived by. They are powerful and purposeful illustrations of what mentoring is all about.

An Invitation to Join an Adventure

Whether you are longing for someone older and wiser to mentor you or you want to use your experience and wisdom to influence others, this book is for you! Read it slowly and thoughtfully. Ask God to help you see the example of Christ more personally than you ever have before. Look up the Scriptures that are suggested and let them speak to you in a direct and intimate way. Invite God to speak to you and guide your thoughts and questions.

If you long to bring the essence of Jesus Christ into the space you occupy, if you desire to influence lives as Jesus did, if you are eager to live for something that will last forever, read on. Come and join me on this adventure!

LEARNING FROM THE MASTER

I asked a sister who worked in Mother Teresa's home how I could be like Mother Teresa. She said, "Mother Teresa simply prays and obeys—daily surrendering moment by moment to Jesus." Anyone can be like her because she is like Jesus, and Jesus desires for each one of us to be like Him.[1]

—LORI SALIERNO

ONE DAY AS I WAS reading my Bible, a statement from the apostle Paul shocked me: "Follow my example, as I follow the example of Christ" (1 Corinthians 11:1, NIV). The words sounded brassy and bold, almost arrogant. How could Paul possibly suggest that people follow his example? Aren't all human beings flawed, at best?

As I studied Paul's life, I came to see this statement in a more positive light. Paul had a dramatic conversion experience on the road to Damascus. His life made a 180-degree turn, and he was transformed by his experience with Christ. I believe that in this verse he was simply saying, "I am trying to follow so closely the example of Christ, keeping my eye on Him, that you can look at me and know how to impact lives as Jesus did."

How in the world can you and I accomplish this? We are flawed, and at times hopelessly imperfect, people. We want to make a difference in the lives of others, but we are so aware of our failings that we don't want others to get close to us. We lack the confidence Paul had. It's easier to follow our to-do list than to allow someone to observe the inconsistencies in what we say and do.

But the remedy may be easier than we might think. Elisabeth Elliot said, "If we demand perfect role models, we will have, except for the Son of Man Himself, none at all."[2] We need to give up our perfectionistic expectations — we will never be a *perfect* reflection of Jesus Christ. The truth is, when we follow Christ's example, we will admit our failures, talk through the growth they produced in our lives, and keep pointing people to Jesus.

I'm encouraged, too, by the wisdom of Southern Baptist author and speaker Esther Burroughs: "You older women of Christ, there is a generation of women out there longing to walk beside you. . . . Mentoring is not about cloning, but about helping women become like Jesus."[3]

Understanding *who* Jesus was and *how* He influenced others during His lifetime can help us learn how we, too, can influence other people on purpose.

THREE FACTS THAT COULD INFLUENCE YOUR LIFE

I've always been fascinated with books on leadership, influence, and personal growth. A few years ago Laurie Beth Jones wrote a book that touched a nerve in many Christians and nonChristians in leadership. Entitled *Jesus CEO: Using Ancient Wisdom for Visionary Leadership*, the book outlined eighty-five specific things Jesus said or did that provide leadership principles for us to follow today. While I don't agree with everything Ms. Jones suggests in her book, I find her foundational premises insightful and thought-provoking.

1. One person trained twelve human beings who went on to so influence the world that time itself is now recorded as being before (B.C.) or after (A.D.) His existence.
2. This person worked with a staff that was totally human and

not divine . . . a staff that in spite of illiteracy, questionable backgrounds, fractious feelings, and momentary cowardice went on to accomplish the tasks He trained them to do. They did this for one main reason—to be with Him again.

3. His leadership style was intended to be put to use by any of us.[4]

Ms. Jones' observations got me to thinking. What would happen if every Christian woman would decide to make a life-changing impact on the lives of at least twelve women within her lifetime? What would happen if we took Christ's example seriously? Even if the results were only a small percentage of what Jesus accomplished, the results would be remarkable.

Jesus influenced individuals from a wide variety of educational and vocational backgrounds. Some were from dysfunctional families. A few were professionals, many were common laborers. Some were fearless, and others lacked courage. However, He saw in each person the potential to become a great leader, and He inspired each one to commit time and energy to learn from Him. He motivated them so much that they longed to be with Him, and even after He ascended into heaven, they carried on His work because they knew they would be with Him again.

As I thought about this, I couldn't help but ask myself the following questions:

- Am I currently available for a season of mentoring to a variety of women from different backgrounds?
- Am I asking God to help me see the potential of the women He wants me to mentor?
- Am I living a life that inspires them to fulfill their purpose?

Jesus' life gives us an example of how to live. His principles for influencing lives are timeless, and more than that, they are available for us to use today.

Am I eager to discover what they are?

Am I willing to be accountable for what I learn?

Have I avoided the responsibility of mentoring others because I feel inadequate?

Will I say to God today, "I will follow You with a pure heart. Show me the people You want me to impact with biblical principles, a listening ear, and encouragement for the journey of life"?

Jesus had only three years of public ministry, but the impact He had on those He mentored still influences you and me today. What can we learn from Him about mentoring?

SEVEN LIFE-CHANGING PRINCIPLES

As I've studied Jesus' example, I've observed seven life-changing principles for making a lasting difference in the lives of those around us.

1. THE PRINCIPLE OF TIME ALONE WITH GOD

By example, Jesus reminds us that the key to spiritual power is time alone with God. Repeatedly we see this scenario in the Gospels: "With the crowd dispersed, he climbed the mountain so he could be by himself and pray. He stayed there alone, late into the night" (Matthew 14:23).

The day before Jesus chose the twelve men He designated as apostles, He spent the night in prayer. The Pharisees and teachers of the Law were looking for a reason to accuse Him. Upset about His Sabbath healings, the Pharisees were discussing what they might do to Jesus.

Instead of running away from the pressure, "[Jesus] climbed a mountain to pray. He was there all night in prayer before God" (Luke 6:12).

Many young Christians struggle with learning how to have a meaningful daily time alone with God. They seem convinced that only spiritual giants are able to maintain a consistent devotional experience, yet they long for more power in their Christian lives and more meaning in their quiet times.

Motivational Christian speaker Becky Tirabassi reminds us of the challenge she experienced when she decided to pray for one hour each day.

> *Just to pray without ceasing for one hour seemed like a monumental achievement in mastering a difficult spiritual discipline, but my deeper walk with Christ has truly been most meaningful to me. Yes, amazing answers to prayer elicit whoops and hollers, and persevering prayer teaches endurance, but spending time with Jesus — perhaps as His disciples did, laughing, crying, complaining, proposing, deliberating, submitting, confessing, and praising — has been the joyful part of our walk together.*[5]

I love the way Becky describes how "normal" spending time with God can be. Just as the disciples talked out loud with Jesus and showed genuine emotion as they told Him their concerns, needs, confessions, and joys, so can we. That's the kind of devotional experience we can encourage younger Christians to develop — a natural conversation with the Person they love the most, and a time of listening to Him through His Word, the Bible.

Becky continues:

> *Had people told me ten, even five years ago that I would be a*
> *prayer motivator, I would not have believed them. . . . Prayer*
> *allows God's presence into all areas and aspects of one's life,*
> *beginning with simple daily decisions and culminating with*
> *one's life's purpose. The combination of prayer and the Word*
> *takes conjecture out of life and replaces it with certainties.*
> *And in the practice of prayer one is escorted farther and*
> *deeper into knowing and loving God.*[6]

If we speak honestly with others about our prayer life, we will tell them about the times when prayer has given us a sense of direction and of God's presence as well as those times when it seems God *hasn't* answered our prayers. When we do this, others are free to speak of their own failures and successes in establishing time with Him.

2. The Principle of Walking and Talking

As we read the Gospels, we discover that much of what Jesus taught the disciples was imparted in a natural, non-classroom environment. He often taught truth through the principle of walking and talking.

One such incident is told in John 9. Jesus and His disciples were walking down the street and saw "a man blind from birth." When the disciples asked if it was this man's or his parents' sin that had caused his blindness, Jesus seized a teachable moment. He said, "You're asking the wrong question. You're looking for someone to blame. There is no such cause-effect here. Look instead for what God can do. We need to be energetically at work for the One who sent me here, working while the sun shines. When night falls, the workday is over" (John 9:3-4).

Then Jesus healed the man's blindness by putting mud on his eyes and telling him to wash in the pool of Siloam. Those who knew this man knew he had been blind since birth. When they asked him what had happened, he told them about Jesus, thus fulfilling Jesus' words, "but this happened so that the work of God might be displayed in his life" (verse 3, NIV). Jesus used this "chance" encounter to warn the disciples about jumping to conclusions or trying to explain the unexplainable. From the text we can infer that the reason the man was born blind was so that God could be glorified. It had nothing to do with the blind man or his family, and everything to do with God. You can be sure this was a lesson not soon forgotten.

Jesus didn't wait for a classroom setting to teach truth to His followers. He used everyday events and interruptions to make truth memorable. He took advantage of what I call "impact moments" — opportunities to teach or influence that are unplanned. Opportunities for impact moments often occurred as Jesus walked with His disciples en route to their next place of ministry. In this same informal way, we can teach and encourage younger Christian women as we drink coffee in their kitchens and give advice on rearing children or as we work in the office or church.

When we intentionally embrace this principle, we will influence others in positive and life-giving ways. Impact moments are not limited to the people with whom we have an ongoing relationship. Remember the story from chapter 1 of Mr. Ottley sparking a desire for God in Meghan's heart? That, too, was an impact moment. When we intentionally embrace the principle of walking and talking, we point others to God and encourage their potential, whether they are friends or strangers.

Jesus knew that most people learn best if we walk beside them instead of ahead of them. Leadership Network sends me a weekly publication that helps Christian leaders make the transition from the present to the future. Through research on individuals born since 1985, the organization has discovered some helpful information. "There has been a real change in how [young people] think, in how they organize and process information. They interact with everything; they have an inability to read just a flat page, and their attention span is short."[7] If this is true, walking and talking — daily relational interaction — may be the best way to reach future generations. Let's use those impact moments to ignite interest in true spirituality!

3. THE PRINCIPLE OF STORYTELLING

One day the disciples came up to Jesus and asked, "Why do you tell stories?" Jesus answered, "You've been given insight into God's kingdom. You know how it works. Not everybody has this gift, this insight; it hasn't been given to them. Whenever someone has a ready heart for this, the insights and understandings flow freely. But if there is no readiness, any trace of receptivity soon disappears. That's why I tell stories: to create readiness, to nudge the people toward receptive insight" (Matthew 13:10-13).

Jesus knew how to capture people's attention. He taught the unknown through the known. He used stories to capture the imaginations of His followers. As a retreat and conference speaker, I've known for a long time that people remember the main point of a message best if it is wrapped in a story they can never forget.

Bill Gove is a professional speaker who has received numerous awards for his speaking excellence, including the National Speakers Association's Cavett Award, which is considered the "Oscar" of public speaking. In The Platform Mastery Workshop, he instructs future speakers with this personal observation: "Good things started to happen to me when I started to see myself as a storyteller, and *not* as a public speaker."[8]

Bill learned the importance of storytelling from Dr. Norman

Vincent Peale. He tells of riding on a train with Dr. Peale after a program and asking, "Dr. Peale, you do this *make a point-tell a story* thing better than anyone in our business." Dr. Peale said, "I had a great teacher," and when I inquired further, he said, "It was Jesus . . . because that's what He did, except in the Bible He called them parables."[9]

The best influencers follow the example of Jesus and use stories to mold minds and hearts and to demonstrate biblical truth.

4. THE PRINCIPLE OF ASKING QUESTIONS

Jesus knew the power of a well-placed question. He didn't ask questions to make Himself look intelligent or to belittle the questioner. His questions were direct, simple, and intriguing; often the type that couldn't be answered with an easy "yes" or "no."

One day Jesus came to the outskirts of Jericho. A blind man sat next to the road asking for handouts. He heard the crowd rustling and asked what was happening. When he was told that Jesus was going by, he yelled, "Jesus! Son of David! Mercy, have mercy on me!" (Luke 18:38). People who were in front of Jesus told the man to be quiet, but he was relentless with his request. Jesus immediately stopped and asked that the man be brought to Him. At that point Jesus asked, "What do you want me to do for you?" (verse 41, NIV).

He told Jesus he wanted to see again and Jesus said, "Go ahead — see again! Your faith has saved and healed you!" (verse 42). The healing was instant, and the man immediately followed Jesus.

Perhaps the most profound question a mentor can ask a mentee is the question Jesus asked: *"What do you want me to do for you?"* By asking that question, Jesus gave the man an opportunity to voice his request and to feel that someone deeply cared about his answer. Jesus also provided an opportunity for the man to verbalize his belief. When we ask questions, we do the same. It keeps us from arriving at premature conclusions about what the person needs or wants. When we ask a woman this question, we allow her to communicate her honest thoughts. When we ask a woman what she wants from us, the answer can take her one step forward to maturity — for she has verbally admitted her need and her desire for change.

At times the person asking the question will be the mentor. Author Bobb Biehl says, "The single most teachable moment of any protégé's life is the few seconds immediately following a sincere question. No curriculum or checklist or theory could replace a mentor's life experience and compassion in such a teachable moment."[10] The biggest growth spurt in a mentoring relationship often takes place when the one being mentored feels comfortable enough with her mentor to ask honest questions.

5. THE PRINCIPLE OF COMPASSION

Jesus gave us a superb demonstration of this important principle through one of His stories. One day He was confronted by a religion scholar who asked, "Teacher, what do I need to do to get eternal life?" (Luke 10:25).

Jesus asked the man to tell Him what was written in God's Law, and he responded, "That you love the Lord your God with all your passion and prayer and muscle and intelligence — and that you love your neighbor as well as you do yourself" (verse 27).

After Jesus told him he gave a good answer, the man queried, "And just how would you define 'neighbor'?" (verse 29). And Jesus answered his question with a story about a man who was traveling from Jerusalem to Jericho. He was attacked and beaten up by robbers on his journey, his clothes were stolen, and he was left half-dead. A priest came by and crossed over to the other side of the road, avoiding the injured man completely. Then a Levite came by and also avoided offering any aid to the man who was hurt.

Finally, a Samaritan came by and "his heart went out to him. He gave him first aid, disinfecting and bandaging his wounds. Then he lifted him onto his donkey, led him to an inn, and made him comfortable. In the morning he took out two silver coins and gave them to the innkeeper, saying, 'Take good care of him. If it costs any more, put it on my bill — I'll pay you on my way back'" (verses 33-35).

Jesus then asked which of the three became a neighbor to the injured man. The scholar responded, "The one who treated him kindly" (Luke 10:37). Jesus told him to go and do the same thing.

I was fascinated with what it means to "treat someone kindly." When I looked up the word *kindly*, I discovered it means not just *showing sympathy*, but demonstrating *hands-on compassion*[11] to a person in need — it's *being Jesus* to someone else. One of the main roles of mentors is to model compassion, to be Jesus to the people we meet today.

Gene Taylor wrote for one of the most popular morning drive-time radio programs in Detroit. Every year his radio station sponsored a local charity, and one year the charitable organization they selected was The Salvation Army. Gene had been away from any organized religion for over ten years when he went on the Salvation Army "Bed and Bread Truck" with the intent of checking it out. Their purpose was to pass out meals and beverages to people who live in the Cass Corridor. This part of Detroit is where the homeless and hurting people of the inner city gather — the prostitutes, the alcohol and drug addicted, and the mentally impaired.

While he was there, he saw an act of compassion that deeply moved him. He watched as a young Salvation Army officer went up to a drunk man and handed him a cup of hot chocolate. The man took the cup in an agitated fashion, and then he swung his arm forward and threw the hot beverage back at her — in her face and all over the front of her uniform. This young woman turned around and poured another cup of hot chocolate, walked up to the *same* man, put her arm around him and said, "Sir, I believe you dropped your hot chocolate. Here, have another."

When Gene and the young woman got back in the truck, he was irate and confused. "I can't believe what I just saw," he ranted. "What are you, some kind of a wimp?" "No," she replied quietly, "I'm some kind of a Christian." Later, Gene asked this woman, "What is it about you that gives you the strength to do what I just saw you do?" She shared the simple gospel message with Gene and spoke passionately of the love of Christ that compelled her to show compassion to others. That single act of loving compassion became a catalyst for a spiritual transformation in his life.

Genuine compassion powerfully affects those who receive it, those who give it, and those who observe it. As women who pour our lives and hearts into younger women, we need to practice compassion.

We can show compassion in practical ways by offering to baby-sit once a week to give a young mother an opportunity to shop, read, or get her hair cut — *alone*. We can see a financial need and purchase a good book or a retreat weekend for a young woman who needs spiritual encouragement. We can invite our mentees to visit a convalescent home with us as we read to older people who can no longer read for themselves and to pray with those who need a reminder of God's love.

Perhaps, most of all, we can take younger women into our arms and hold them when they feel hopeless, and remind them we care about them. This example, more than anything else, will teach them to do the same for others. A theologian once said, "What value has compassion that does not take its object in its arms?"[12] Being *Jesus* to someone else is a hands-on principle. And sometimes, like the young Salvation Army officer, we may have an opportunity to share Jesus with someone who understands the love of Christ because they first observed genuine compassion in us.

6. THE PRINCIPLE OF UNCONDITIONAL LOVE

Jesus practiced the kind of love that doesn't come naturally. In John 8 the scribes and Pharisees brought a woman to Him who had been caught in adultery. The Bible says, "They stood her in plain sight of everyone and said, 'Teacher, this woman was caught red-handed in the act of adultery. Moses, in the Law, gives orders to stone such persons. What do you say?'" (John 8:4-5).

Jesus paused and wrote in the dirt while the religion scholars continued to badger Him. Then He said, "The sinless one among you, go first: Throw the stone" (verse 7). After hearing His words, the men walked away, leaving Him alone with the woman.

Jesus asked the woman where her accusers were and if anyone had condemned her. She responded: "No one, Master." "Neither do I," said Jesus. "Go on your way. From now on, don't sin" (verse 11).

Jesus reminds us to love and forgive those who have been caught in sin. He further reminds us to point them in the right direction. "Don't sin," He says to us and to the woman in the story.

When we have blown it, even in small ways, it's natural to question our worth. Most women I know tell me they have questioned their significance at some point in their life. This feeling might go back to a negative nickname, to an imperfect body part (most of us have a few), a time of walking away from God, or being rejected by a parent, teacher, sibling, friend, or husband. When we feel unloved, unwanted, and unworthy, no other success in life makes up for the empty void inside.

When you help a younger woman know who she is in Him — that God *delights* in her — her worth is validated, and she can begin the journey toward a thriving love relationship with Jesus. There will be times when you may be disappointed in the choices she makes, and that's when you need to live out the principle of unconditional love, no strings attached. A person's actions may not always warrant your support, but her potential does!

Zephaniah 3:17 reminds us: "He will take great delight in you, he will quiet you with his love, he will rejoice over you with singing" (NIV). Women of Faith speaker Marilyn Meberg says, "Knowing He delights in us allows us to feel secure about who we are and Whose we are."[13]

7. THE PRINCIPLE OF CASTING VISION

Between the time of His resurrection and His ascension into heaven, Jesus cast His vision of what His followers should do in His absence:

> *"Go out and train everyone you meet, far and near, in this way of life, marking them by baptism in the threefold name: Father, Son, and Holy Spirit. Then instruct them in the practice of all I have commanded you. I'll be with you as you do this, day after day after day, right up to the end of the age." (Matthew 28:19-20)*

Jesus made sure His followers knew what He wanted them to do — and history and Scripture tell us He succeeded in motivating them to carry it out!

Great influencers know how to nurture the potential in others to fulfill their God-given purpose. They paint a verbal picture of what God can do with the life of another, and they help the protégé to see how invaluable her part is in building the kingdom of God. This can be done by providing education, answers to questions, and networking opportunities; validating her unique giftedness; and affirming what she is doing right.

Much-loved pastor Bill Hybels says, "If there is anything I have learned over the years at Willow Creek Community Church, it is to never underestimate how often I need to rekindle the vision . . . to consistently reeducate people why we are on the track we are on . . . why we do things the way we do."[14] That's exactly what a mentor does.

THE TEACHABLE HEART

If you dare to read further, you may be at risk for becoming a Christ-follower who cannot go through a day without influencing someone else's life like He did. This book is not for the chicken-hearted; it's for the courageous woman who is ready to risk a couple of setbacks, and perhaps a failure or two, in order to set her course in the direction of helping others to square with biblical principles. Let's get going!

Chapter Three

THE PRINCIPLE OF TIME ALONE WITH GOD

The thing that made praying an hour a day work for me is that I write out my prayers. This is relational and tangible. I'm talking to my best friend, which I have no problem ever doing.[1]

— BECKY TIRABASSI

FOR YEARS I RACED FROM one meeting or activity to another because I hated being alone. I equated solitude with loneliness. It made me feel worthless and uncomfortable. To me, a productive life consisted of a full calendar and constant interaction. However, the more things I put into my schedule, the less happy I became. And there were times when I felt used by people I loved because the more I did, the more they expected me to do.

After our son, Jason Paul, was born, I decided to leave teaching and become a stay-at-home mom. That time was incredibly difficult for me. I loved my baby, but I missed feeling "important" as an award-winning teacher. One day I spent an afternoon with one of my mentors, and she spoke of looking forward to the next day because her calendar had *nothing* on it. She told me she regularly scheduled these open days in her life to spend a quiet day alone with God. She smiled when I asked what she could possibly find to do with Him . . . alone . . . *all day*.

She spent the rest of the afternoon telling me how she and God spent their days together. She talked as if God were her best friend. As I was about to leave, she told me, "My days with Him — especially when the interruptions are minimal — are my favorite days." I knew she meant it. I left excited about scheduling time alone with God. I knew I had a lot to learn, but this was a beginning.

I've come a long way since then, and I'm convinced that time alone with God is non-negotiable if we want to be like Jesus and to influence others like He did.

LEARNING FROM THE MASTER

What can we learn from Jesus about spending time alone with God?

IT WAS A PRIORITY

No matter how busy He was, Jesus spent time alone with His Father. In Mark 1:21-35 we are given a glimpse of twenty-four hours in the life of Christ. He was in Capernaum and began that Sabbath day by preaching in the synagogue. While He was speaking, a demon-possessed man caused a disruption. Jesus spoke with authority and cast out the evil spirit, amazing the crowd, who had never seen anything like this before.

After leaving the synagogue, He went with James and John to the home of Simon and Andrew where He healed Simon's mother-in-law of a fever. That same day, after sunset, people brought their sick and demon-possessed friends and relatives to Jesus. In fact, "The whole town gathered at the door, and Jesus healed many who had various diseases. He also drove out many demons" (Mark 1:33-34, NIV).

I'm out of breath just thinking about all Jesus did that day: preaching, casting out demons, traveling to the home of Simon and Andrew (while talking to James and John), healing Simon's mother-in-law, and ministering to the many who showed up on the doorstep. I would have pulled the shades and turned out the lights. Not Jesus. He walked out the door and "cured their sick bodies and tormented spirits" (Mark 1:34).

After such a day, we wouldn't be surprised if Jesus took the next few days off, but He didn't: "Very early in the morning, while it was still dark, Jesus got up, left the house and went off to a solitary place, where he prayed" (Mark 1:35, NIV). After the busiest day in the recorded history of the life of Christ, He got up early so He could enjoy the presence of His Father. He didn't let a hectic schedule crowd out His time alone with God.

TALKING WITH HIS FATHER HELPED TO CLARIFY HIS MISSION

Jesus seemed energized by spending time alone with God. When Simon and his companions found Jesus, they said, "Everybody's looking for you!" Jesus' immediate reaction was enthusiastic: "Let's go to the rest of the villages so I can preach there also." I sense in His response a renewed passion in spite of the draining circumstances. He also came back from His time of prayer with a clear sense of His mission: "This is why I've come" (Mark 1:37-38).

Several years ago I accepted the position of director of women's ministries in my church. There were many volunteers who worked on various committees within the ministry, but I began targeting two key young women, Sarah and Nancy. I met with them and asked if they would pray about being the coordinators of the two outreach events we have for women each year. We wanted to provide a program that would be enjoyable and interesting for unchurched women, but that also would effectively present the gospel message.

I didn't ask for an immediate commitment, but I requested that they think about this opportunity for ministry and then pray individually and together about it. Before we parted, I prayed and asked God to give them a clear picture of His vision for their immediate future.

After two weeks, they made an appointment to see me. Their radiant faces reflected their answer. Prayer had clarified their mission. Not only did they tell me yes, they told me of unchurched friends and relatives they were planning to invite. Had they committed to working on this project too quickly, they might have questioned the timing and resented the amount of work involved. However, prayer helped them focus on the aim of these events — reaching nonChristians with the gospel message — and it confirmed their personal commitment to evangelism.

TIME IN PRAYER PRODUCES RESULTS

Jesus had been making a circuit of all the towns and villages, connecting with many people. He taught in their meeting places, reported kingdom news, and healed diseased bodies and hurt lives: "When he looked out over the crowds, his heart broke. So confused and aimless they were, like sheep with no shepherd. 'What a huge harvest!' he said to his disciples. 'How few workers! On your knees and pray for harvest hands!'" (Matthew 9:36-38).

Everywhere Jesus went, something exciting and spiritually refreshing was taking place. Everywhere Jesus looked, He saw more people with heavy hearts and deep needs. His heart broke, and He pleaded with the disciples to see how big the task was and how few people there were to help.

He doesn't say, "You *must* get involved in this ministry! If *you* don't do it, no one else will." There's no pressure or guilt trip laid on anybody. But Christ is passionate as He pleads with them to get on their knees and pray for harvest hands. And the result was immediate. "The prayer was no sooner prayed than it was answered. Jesus called twelve of his followers and sent them into the ripe fields" (Matthew 10:1). As they prayed for harvest hands, some of those who were following Jesus felt God calling *them* to be the workers. They became the answer to their own prayer! Prayer always produces results. It's not always in the way we expect, but there are always results.

In my early years of teaching a Bible Study Fellowship class, I realized God was calling me to travel in conference and retreat ministry, which would mean giving up my teaching position. It was a large class, and we wondered who God wanted to teach after I left. I met with the discussion leaders weekly for prayer, study, and encouragement, and asked them to pray about who should take this position.

I had been spending time informally with one of the women in this group. Sandy had a powerful personal testimony, a love for God's Word, a belief in the power of prayer, and a desire to teach others, but she felt inadequate to take my place. As we prayed — week after week — I could see God confirming to her, through His Word and through the wise counsel of godly leaders, that she was the answer to our prayers. Sandy became the answer to her own prayer for a teacher for the class.

Jesus Often Went to a Solitary Place to Be Alone with God

Jesus often left the company of the disciples and dismissed the crowd to meet with His Father. As the Gospel writer in Luke 5:16 said, "But Jesus often withdrew to lonely places and prayed" (NIV). I am always amazed that Jesus seemed to find a place to pray where He was alone.

As busy as our lives are, sometimes a solitary place is hard to come by — and that's where creativity comes in. Because I am frequently in my car (I live one-and-a-half hours from the nearest airport), my automobile has become one of my "solitary places." While I'm driving, I'm spending time alone with God. I usually begin this time by playing a CD of praise and worship music. As I sing with the recorded music, I worship my Creator and my spirit is lifted, even in the middle of stop-and-go traffic! I converse with God about my husband — the good things and the irritating things. I talk about my concerns for our son. I tell God all my hopes and dreams as well as my disappointments and fears. I ask for wisdom about decisions, and I ask Him to continue to make me more like Jesus. If I pass an accident or if an ambulance passes me, I pray for the people who may be hurt and in need of assistance, both physical and spiritual. My trips in the car have made it a solitary place to spend time alone with God, even though my eyes are wide open.

Other women I know listen to Scripture or sermon CDs while riding alone in a car. This allows them to quiet their hearts and to keep their focus on God, listening for His voice in Scripture or in the words of one of His children.

Some of you may be responding, "But Carol, I have two children under the age of five. There are *no* solitary places in my house. Being alone is impossible. Private time for prayer or Bible reading does not exist at my house." I heard about one mother of preschoolers who let her children play on the floor in the family room while *she* got into the playpen for her time alone with God. I don't know how effective that was, but I do think it's important to plan ahead for occasional blocks of time alone with Him.

Marlae Gritter, the national director of coordinators for Moms in Touch International, encourages women to plan ahead for occasional "DAWG days" (Day Alone With God). It's a day when you schedule time with Him. It might be two hours, a full morning, or a complete day when you spend time alone with God. The location might be in your own home or at a park, retreat center, or library.

The structure can vary: Bible study, prayer, listening to what God says to your heart, singing or worship, reading a chapter of an inspiring biography or a book on spiritual discipline or Christian leadership. If you have young children, good friends can trade child care responsibilities to free each other for the opportunity of enjoying God in solitude. These days can be renewing, spiritually challenging, and essential for maintaining balance.

But don't be limited by the common definition of a "solitary place." I believe a solitary place is a state of mind that allows us to listen to God's voice in spite of outward chaos. In his book *Celebration of Discipline*, Richard Foster says:

> *There is a solitude of the heart that can be maintained at all times. Crowds or the lack of them have little to do with this inward attentiveness. . . . Inward solitude will have outward manifestations. There will be the freedom to be alone, not in order to be away from people but in order to hear better. Jesus lived in inward "heart solitude." . . . We must seek out the recreating stillness of solitude if we want to be with others meaningfully.*[2]

A "solitude of the heart" can be maintained when our focus is on Him and our activities are monitored by an awareness of His presence. After I began practicing this discipline, I noticed changes in my daily responses to normal events. When the phone rang, I prayed for the person I was about to talk to, even before I knew who it was. When the woman in front of me at the supermarket had her credit card rejected, instead of being impatient because the delay was taking my time, I prayed for her.

INSTRUCTIONS ON HOW TO PRAY

Jesus gave us some very specific instructions regarding the best way to spend time alone with God.

Don't put on airs to impress God. "And when you come before God, don't turn that into a theatrical production either. All these people making a regular show out of their prayers, hoping for stardom! Do you think God sits in a box seat?" (Matthew 6:5).

Find a secluded place to pray; keep your prayers simple and honest. "Here's what I want you to do: Find a quiet, secluded place so you won't be tempted to role-play before God. Just be there as simply and honestly as you can manage. The focus will shift from you to God, and you will begin to sense his grace" (Matthew 6:6). I think sensing His grace is what solitude of the heart feels like.

Talk to God as your loving Father; don't follow the formulas and techniques of others. "The world is full of so-called prayer warriors who are prayer-ignorant. They're full of formulas and programs and advice, peddling techniques for getting what you want from God. Don't fall for that nonsense. This is your Father you are dealing with, and he knows better than you what you need. With a God like this loving you, you can pray very simply" (Matthew 6:7-9).

When you fast, don't do it to impress people. "When you practice some appetite-denying discipline [fast] to better concentrate on God, don't make a production out of it. It might turn you into a small-time celebrity but it won't make you a saint. If you 'go into training' inwardly, act normal outwardly. Shampoo and comb your hair, brush your teeth, wash your face. God doesn't require attention-getting devices. He won't overlook what you are doing; he'll reward you well" (Matthew 6:16-18).

It's interesting to note that Jesus did not say "*if* you fast" or "you *must* fast." He said, "*When* you fast." This verse leads us to believe that He assumes believers *will* fast and that they needed to know how to do it properly. Jesus taught that fasting was not a discipline that should ever be used to impress others with our spirituality. It's between Him and you — no one else.

There is a time for celebration and a time for fasting. One day John the Baptist's followers approached Jesus and asked, "'Why is it that we and the Pharisees rigorously discipline body and spirit by fasting, but your followers don't?' Jesus told them, 'When you're celebrating a wedding, you don't skimp on the cake and wine. You feast. Later you may need to pull in your belt, but not now. No one throws cold water on a friendly bonfire. This is Kingdom Come!'" (Matthew 9:14-15).

I think Jesus was saying that there's a time to fast and a time to celebrate. It wouldn't be physically, spiritually, or emotionally healthy to fast every day, but it's important to do it at the right time. Many Christians fast during times of crisis or when they need God's guidance for a particular decision.

Several years ago I was invited to be a guest on a television program. The host was a remarkable woman with a doctorate in educational psychology and a warm, charismatic personality. The live telecast went well, and we both enjoyed our time in the studio together. We decided to meet later, and I invited her to join me for dinner at my hotel because I was on a ministry assignment in her hometown. She politely declined dinner but set a time for us to meet later.

During our meeting she told me she hoped she had not appeared rude when she turned down my invitation to dinner, but she was fasting and felt it would be inappropriate to meet at mealtime when she was not eating. I asked her about the purpose of the fast and discovered that this godly woman had been married to a pastor, but they were separated, and he had given absolutely no hope of reconciliation. She was praying for a miracle that God would "resurrect and restore" the relationship and the marriage, but nothing seemed to be happening. With an urgent need to know the mind of God more clearly, to be drawn into a closer relationship with Him, and to discern what action (if any) to take now, she felt led to enter an extended period of prayer and fasting. Previously in her Christian walk, she had fasted for brief periods and had experienced tremendous spiritual power and a deeper walk with the Father.

Her face was radiant as she spoke to me of this intimate encounter with God. Instead of a bitter, downtrodden woman who had been dumped by her husband, she was a model of strength, beauty, intelligence, and deep spirituality. She didn't know it, but she was teaching me about the benefit and importance of fasting. She gave me literature, encouragement, and advice on how to integrate this discipline into my own prayer life. It was an impact moment in my life.

Many authors who write on spiritual disciplines have commented that the benefits of fasting include a greater power in intercessory prayer, physical well-being, a sense of "balance" in life regarding letting go of nonessentials, wisdom in decisions, and deliverance for people in bondage. Author Wesley Duewel says, "Fasting is God's chosen way to deepen and strengthen prayer. . . . biblical fasting is a form of self-denial for the sake of Jesus and His kingdom. It is a deliberate abstinence from some or all food for a spiritual purpose. It demands a deep level of commitment and sacrifice."[3]

I admit I'm still learning to practice this discipline, but the spiritual power attained through fasting and prayer is so essential that we must be open to practicing it ourselves and to encouraging others to do so as well.

"WHEN YOU PRAY, SAY . . ."

One day the disciples observed Jesus in prayer and overheard His intimate conversation with God. As soon as Jesus finished praying, one of the disciples said, "Master, teach us to pray just as John taught his disciples" (Luke 11:1).

Chuck Swindoll comments on this:

> *What a fascinating request! The disciples lived in a religious culture that promoted prayer. They had heard people pray at the temple in Jerusalem . . . and in countless synagogue services. Before spending time with Jesus, I suspect each disciple would have thought he knew how to pray. But when they watched Jesus pray, they saw an intimacy, a fervency, a level of effectiveness that made their prayers seem feeble in comparison. With such a model before them, they wanted to learn how to pray like He did!*[4]

In response, Jesus prays the Lord's Prayer, and offers us an example of how we can talk to God when we spend time alone with Him. In *The Message*, Eugene Peterson brings us a fresh understanding of the wording of this well-known passage in Luke 11:2-4.

Let's take a closer look at each portion of this prayer and how we can use it to teach others how to pray.

"Father." I encourage women to acknowledge that God is their precious, awesome, *Abba* Father, their own dear daddy — a personal, loving, and compassionate Father.

"Reveal who you are." Pray that God will show Himself to you through His Word, other Christians, the circumstances in your day, and the challenges you face. I sometimes tell women about the specific ways God has revealed Himself to me through a combination of His Word, circumstances, and the wise counsel of godly people.

"Set the world right." Pray for our governmental leaders and for our country. As you listen to the radio or watch the news, pray for those you see pictured in war-torn areas in Third World countries or in countries devastated by earthquakes, tsunamies, and hurricanes. I try to discuss current events with women I'm mentoring and will sometimes pray aloud with them about specific needs that are currently in the news.

"Keep us alive with three square meals." Thank God for the food that sustains your life and pray for those who are hungry. Because we often share meals with those we mentor, expressing appreciation to God for more than adequate amounts of food is something I do regularly with younger Christians.

"Keep us forgiven with you and forgiving others." Confess any sin in your life and pray for people who have wronged you. I sometimes confess my sins with women I'm mentoring, if and when it seems helpful and appropriate. If we are going to teach others the importance of forgiveness, it is important that we don't hold grudges or harbor resentment toward those who may have hurt us.

"Keep us safe from ourselves and the Devil." Pray that God will keep you from temptation and aware of the power of God over the Enemy. I

often tell people that I pray for a circle of angels to protect our family, whether we are together or apart. When I pray aloud about that, it encourages those I mentor to pray that way for their families.

The follow-up instruction Jesus gives emphasizes the importance of being intentional and fervent when we pray.

PERSONAL AND DIRECT

With God, prayer is not a "cat-and-mouse game"; it is personal and it is powerful.

Jesus tells us, "Don't bargain with God. Be direct. Ask for what you need. This is not a cat-and-mouse, hide-and-seek game we're in.... Don't you think the Father who conceived you in love will give the Holy Spirit when you ask him?" (Luke 11:10-11).

Probably the most fervent, specific prayer Jesus ever uttered was in the Garden of Gethsemane. Jesus went with His disciples to Gethsemane and asked them to stay there while He went to pray. He took Peter, James, and John with Him. The Bible says He was sorrowful and troubled. With urgency, He says, "This sorrow is crushing my life out. Stay here and keep vigil with me" (Matthew 26:38). He went a little further and fell prostrate on the ground and prayed, "My Father, if there is any way, get me out of this. But please, not what I want. You, what do *you* want?" (verse 39).

Jesus came back to His disciples and found them sound asleep. He said to Peter, "Can't you stick it out with me a single hour? Stay alert; be in prayer so you don't wander into temptation without even knowing you're in danger" (verses 40-41).

He left them a second time and prayed, "My Father, if there is no other way than this, drinking this cup to the dregs, I'm ready. Do it your way" (verse 42).

Jesus came back to the disciples and found them asleep *again*. Jesus must have felt lonely and fearful of the future. His prayers had been intense, personal, and direct.

A few years ago I heard the testimony of Jim Cymbala, pastor of the Brooklyn Tabernacle. About twenty-five years ago he became the pastor of a dying church in a rough neighborhood in Brooklyn, New York. There were a handful of people left in the congregation and in his first month as pastor there was a financial crisis: They could not pay the $232 mortgage payment. Jim's response is recorded in his book, *Fresh Wind, Fresh Fire*.

> I went upstairs, sat at my little desk, put my head down, and began to cry. "God," I sobbed, "what can I do? We can't even pay the mortgage."
>
> That night was the midweek service, and I knew there wouldn't be more than three or four people attending. The offering would probably be less than ten dollars. How was I going to get through this?
>
> I cried out to the Lord for a full hour or so. Eventually, I dried my tears—and a new thought came. Wait a minute! Besides the mail slot in the front door, the church also has a post office box. I'll go across the street and see what's there. Surely God will answer my prayer!
>
> With renewed confidence I walked across the street, crossed the post office lobby, and twirled the knob on the little box. I peered inside.

Nothing.

As I stepped back into the sunshine, trucks roared down Atlantic Avenue. If one had flattened me just then, I wouldn't have felt any lower. Was God abandoning us? Was I doing something that displeased Him? I trudged wearily back across the street to the little building.

As I unlocked the door, I was met with another surprise. There on the foyer floor was something that hadn't been there just three minutes earlier: a simple white envelope. No address, no stamp—nothing. Just a white envelope.

With trembling hands I opened it to find . . . two $50 bills.

I began shouting all by myself in the empty church. "God, you came through! You came through!" We had $160 in the bank, and with this $100 we could make the mortgage payment. My soul let out a deep "Hallelujah!" What a lesson for a disheartened young pastor!

To this day I don't know where that money came from. I only know it was a sign to me that God was near—and faithful.[5]

Jim Cymbala became such a believer in prayer that he declared to his congregation, "From this day on, the prayer meeting will be the barometer of our church. What happens on Tuesday night will be the gauge by which we will judge success or failure, because that will be the measure by which God blesses us. . . . [Prayer] will be the engine that will drive the church."[6]

Like Jesus, this man asked for what he needed; he continued to seek an answer when nothing looked promising, and he knocked on the heart of God.

INFLUENCING OTHERS TO
SPEND TIME WITH GOD

As I've already pointed out, Jesus not only lived the seven life-changing principles covered in this book, He taught them as well. If we are to shape hearts into His image, we must do the same. Some women who read this book, however, may not feel ready or "called" to engage in a formal mentoring relationship — and that's okay. Remember the results of the survey that I mentioned in chapter 1? Many godly men and women had no formal mentoring relationships; instead, they were influenced by impact moments. If you desire to influence others to become like Christ, you can ask God to help you become sensitive to impact moments in which you can impart these principles. As you study these principles and seek to live them out, you will begin to influence others in life-giving ways.

Others of you *do* feel God is calling you to enter into a mentoring relationship. In fact, you have already spotted that "younger woman with potential." If so, begin with friendship. It might frighten a young woman to think of entering into a "formal" mentoring relationship when first approached, so start with a relationship that offers a listening ear and wise counsel in a setting that makes communication feel unthreatening. Once a comfortable relationship has been established and a level of trust is developed, you can talk with her about consistently meeting with you for a period of time. If she agrees, Bible study and prayer should play a vital role in your time together. As she grows stronger in her faith, she will spend time alone with God, following the same procedure she's been taught.

Here are some ways to intentionally impart this principle.

Tell Others What God Is Teaching You in Your Time with Him

When our son was a young naval officer, he was once given an assignment that would put him in extreme physical danger. Just as I was wrestling with being fearful for my son's life, I came to Philippians 4:6-7: "Don't fret or worry. Instead of worrying, pray. Let petitions and praises shape your worries into prayers, letting God know your concerns. Before you know it, a sense of God's wholeness, everything coming together for good, will come and settle you down. It's wonderful what happens when Christ displaces worry at the center of your life."

The next day I was meeting with a young woman, and as I asked her to pray with me, I told her of my fear and of the encouragement I'd found in this passage. As we prayed together, I chose to put my worries in God's hands, and I sensed a growing awareness that God designed my son to be a person who thrives on adventure, personal challenge, and being an aggressive problem solver. Through prayer I gradually was able to release my son and take my "controlling" worries off his life and free him to live out the design God intended for him. (In case you're wondering, I have had to do this more than once. Sometimes daily!)

Pray Out Loud Together

A friend who came to know the Lord as an adult told me about her first experience of praying with a small group of believers. She said as one person was praying aloud, others in the group were making humming and grunting sounds. It took her a few minutes to realize that people in this prayer group were verbalizing their agreement with the one who was praying. She said, "I grew to love this *holy grunting*." Talking about these things in a relaxed, sometimes humorous way takes the pressure out of the situation and releases others to risk praying aloud.

If you are meeting with someone formally, talk to God together every time you meet. Before you pray, write down any new specific prayer requests she has for herself or her family. If she is reluctant to pray aloud, describe your early fears regarding prayer and help her to see how natural it is to speak aloud to your Best Friend.

SING PRAISE AND WORSHIP SONGS TOGETHER

Judy told me that several years ago her husband had lost his job, and his prospects for immediate employment looked dim. Their spirits were low and their financial outlook was bleak. On that very day Luci, her friend and encourager, had called. After grieving "heart-to-heart" about the disappointments and hurts Judy was experiencing, Luci said, "Let's sing together over the phone. Let's sing 'It is Well with My Soul.'"[7]

I sing in the car, in the shower, and when I'm outside walking. Sometimes I use a hymn book when I'm spending time alone with God and sing a song of praise directly to my Father. Some of my most precious times with women I'm mentoring are when one of us quietly begins singing a song that matches the theme of our conversation and prayers.

DISCUSS THE BOOKS AND ARTICLES YOU ARE READING AND SUGGEST READING MATERIAL

Just this week I was reading Philip Yancey's award-winning book *The Jesus I Never Knew*. I had been trying to get a clearer picture of who God is — personal, relational, and nonintimidating. I got so excited about the book, I called a young friend I'm encouraging in her walk with God and said, "Listen to this!"

> *Books of theology tend to define God by what He is not: God is immortal, invisible, infinite. But what is God like, positively? . . . God, is, in a word, Christlike. Jesus presents a God with skin on whom we can take or leave, love or ignore. . . . Brilliant, untamed, tender, creative, slippery, irreducible, paradoxically humble — Jesus stands up to scrutiny. He is who I want my God to be.*[8]

Jesus was God in the flesh; when we study Jesus, we are discovering who God is in all of His love, compassion, grace, and mercy.

When we enthusiastically verbalize our fresh insights from books and periodicals we are reading, it can encourage others to read excellent material on the same subjects.

PRACTICE! PRACTICE! PRACTICE!

It was a sunny afternoon and Marlee was busy making enchiladas for dinner when her young daughter, Lea, asked how she knew when God was speaking to her and how she knew it was His voice. Marlee had often told her children to listen to God. The conversation went like this:

"But do you hear Him talking into your ears?" Lea asked.

"No it's a new way of hearing."

"Well, then, how do you know for sure?"

It takes practice. . . . You know how Grandpa asks you to close your eyes and open your hands before he gives you a treat? . . . You hold out empty hands. . . . Your eyes close out all distractions. . . . (It's like that with God.) . . . Just before God speaks, God Himself is more important than anything He's going to say. His silence speaks loudest of all. Then, when you hear His voice, you know.[9]

The more you listen, read His Word, pray, sing, and delight in Him, the more it becomes as automatic as breathing.

Chapter Four

THE PRINCIPLE OF WALKING AND TALKING

Walking with Christ is just that—a walk. I know I'm not perfect, and I try not to be disappointed in myself. . . . I meet with a group of women on Friday mornings. We don't call it a Bible study, but we talk about the Bible and discuss other books that deal with living out your Christian faith in today's world. These women are always there for me, and that's a great source of strength.[1]

— MARILYN QUAYLE

J UDY HAMPTON FELT CONSPICUOUS ON her first evening of attending choir practice at a new church. She had made her way to a vacant seat in the second row when she was immediately summoned by a woman with a huge smile who said, "Please, come and sit by me." As Judy slipped into the seat, Tutty introduced herself and said, "Tell me how you came to this church, and tell me all about you and your family."

A few days after choir practice, Tutty invited Judy to her home. Upon arriving, Judy discovered she was the honored guest. Tutty had invited several of her friends, including her sister, Mary Ann, to this event for the purpose of introducing them to Judy. From that day on, Tutty and Mary Ann began teaching Judy from their lives.

Tutty is in heaven now, but Judy clearly remembers the influence these two women had on her life.

> *I didn't grow up in a Christian home, and the Christian life was new to me. I needed mature women to teach, model, and disciple me, but never in my wildest dreams did I know it could be so much fun! Both Mary Ann and Tutty modeled the virtues of being a Christian woman. They invited me into their lives. They taught me about hospitality. I saw firsthand how they embraced their*

roles as wives and mothers. They gave of their time and resources. They imparted the truths from the Bible by living them in front of me (not by preaching), and put up with my endless stream of questions and desperate phone calls seeking answers. Their contagious love for Christ inspired me to seek Him every day.

If we waited for formal teaching moments to make a difference in the lives of others, most of us would miss the opportunities we have to "be Jesus" to the people we have the privilege of influencing. Whether they realized it or not, these two dear women had impacted Judy's life through the principle of walking and talking.

LEARNING FROM THE MASTER

Jesus spent three years in His public ministry walking and talking with His disciples. He didn't have the luxury of formally teaching His disciples in a seminary classroom. His closest followers walked with Him from town to town — they went everywhere He went. Whether He was teaching the disciples, visiting friends like Martha and Mary, or responding to a touch from someone in the crowd, Jesus made every contact count. The most important life lessons are almost always "caught" rather than "taught." Knowing this, Jesus took advantage of impact moments to teach and influence others, including those with whom He had chance or ordinary encounters.

How did Jesus demonstrate this principle?

JESUS TURNED INTERRUPTIONS INTO SIGNIFICANT APPOINTMENTS

One day an important man named Jairus came up to Jesus. He fell at Jesus' feet and begged Him to come to his home because his only child, his twelve-year-old daughter, was dying. Jesus went with him and worked his way through the pressing crowd. However, there was a woman in that jostling crowd who had been struggling with hemorrhages for twelve years. She had already spent all of her resources on medical advice and on physicians who hadn't helped her condition. Working her way through the mass of people, she slipped in behind Jesus and touched the edge of his robe. The Bible says, "At that very moment her hemorrhaging stopped. Jesus said, 'Who touched me?'" (Luke 8:44-45).

When no one stepped forward, Peter insisted that in a crowd of that size, dozens of people would have touched Him. But Jesus knew the difference between the press of the crowd and the touch of faith, and He asked the woman to identify herself. She knew she could no longer remain hidden, and she knelt in front of Him, trembling. Then she told her story—both why she touched Him and how, at that very moment, she had experienced healing. Jesus said, "Daughter, you took a risk trusting me, and now you're healed and whole. Live well, live blessed!" (Luke 8:48). Following this incident, Jesus went to Jairus's home and brought his daughter back to life. Jesus used this "interruption" to demonstrate that faith heals. This impact moment also taught the disciples that no person is more important to Jesus than another. The daughter of a community leader was dying, but Jesus took the time to heal a woman in the crowd.

My friend Nan Walker once answered the phone call of a marketing analyst who wanted ten minutes of her time to answer survey questions.

Instead of replying that she didn't have time and hanging up quickly, she said, "I'll answer your questions if you'll answer two of mine." To her surprise, the person conducting the survey agreed to her unusual request. After the survey was completed, the marketing analyst said, "Now I'd like to hear your questions."

When Nan asked the two questions, the answers revealed that the person she was speaking to had no relationship with Jesus Christ and no hope of eternal life. So Nan asked if she could share how she came to experience personal faith in Christ and a sense of hope about the future. She explained how the woman taking the survey could have this same hope. By the end of the phone call, the analyst prayed with Nan and invited Christ into her life. By example, Nan mentored me in the art of turning interruptions into important appointments.

JESUS "HUNG OUT" IN PEOPLE'S HOMES

One day Jesus entered a village and went to the home of Martha and Mary. Martha welcomed Him and made Him feel at home before she headed to the kitchen to prepare a meal. Her sister, Mary, "sat before the Master, hanging on every word he said" (Luke 10:39). Martha came back into the room from the kitchen and interrupted Jesus and Mary. She said, "Master, don't you care that my sister has abandoned the kitchen to me? Tell her to lend me a hand" (verse 40).

Jesus said, "Martha, dear Martha, you're fussing far too much and getting yourself worked up over nothing. One thing only is essential, and Mary has chosen it — it's the main course, and won't be taken from her" (verse 41). Even though Jesus was relaxing in a friend's home, He made every minute count. Here He is teaching the importance of *being* over *doing*. Mary seemed to understand that who we are is more important to Jesus than what we do for Him.

As the oldest of six preacher's kids, I've always felt sorry for Martha because so many of the meal preparations for large groups of people coming to the parsonage were part of my responsibilities. I grew up feeling the urgency of "doing" and for years I called my perfectionism "a pursuit of excellence."

After we were married, Gene and I sometimes invited company for dinner or for a weekend in our home. I was always spending too much time on what the table looked like and on how perfectly the meals were orchestrated. By the time the guests arrived, I was tired and stressed. Making this much work out of having company didn't make me want to entertain very often and made me cranky and irritable around my family.

I remember admitting to Chris, a young woman I often invited into my home, that I had been a *screaming monster*, a *silent martyr*, and a *skillful pretender* during the past because I'd been trying to impress houseguests. Behind closed doors I'd yelled at my husband, I'd been impatient with my son, and then I'd put on a big smile just in time for church (and to greet our guests) as I pretended everything was *fine*. I was fuming on the inside, while on the outside I was talking to my husband during mealtime with our guests — just enough so they wouldn't guess I was angry with him, but so he knew I was still ticked off.

I described this unpleasant scenario to Chris and told her of my need to apologize to my husband and son and ask for their forgiveness for my lethal attitude and hurtful behavior. She looked at me with an expression of shock on her face and haltingly said, "I always thought you had a *perfect* marriage and that you were an *ideal* mother. It made me think I could never be good enough to get close to you. But now, I think we could be friends." By opening my heart and home to Chris, I taught her that God was still molding me into His image. Most surprising, I learned that being vulnerable about my sins and weaknesses made me a more desirable person to get to know.

JESUS TOOK HIS DISCIPLES WITH HIM WHEN HE TRAVELED AND PREACHED

"Jesus made a circuit of all the towns and villages. He taught in their meeting places, reported kingdom news, and healed their diseased bodies, healed their bruised and hurt lives" (Matthew 9:35). Every day for three years Jesus allowed His followers to accompany Him while He traveled, preached, healed, told stories, taught object lessons, and gave instruction. Check out just a few of the passages in which we see this scenario:

> *Coming down off the mountain with them, he stood on a plain surrounded by disciples, and was soon joined by a huge congregation from all over Judea and Jerusalem. . . . They had come both to hear him and to be cured of their ailments. . . . Everyone was trying to touch him—so much energy surging from him, so many people healed! Then he spoke: "You're blessed when you've lost it all. God's kingdom is there for the finding." (Luke 6:17-20)*

> *He continued according to plan, traveled to town after town, village after village, preaching God's kingdom, spreading the Message. The Twelve were with him. (Luke 8:1)*

As the disciples spent time with Jesus, they were able to see that He both "walked and talked" His message. For example:

> *People brought babies to Jesus, hoping he might touch them. When the disciples saw it, they shooed them off. Jesus called them back. "Let these children alone. Don't get between them and me. These children are the kingdom's pride and joy. Mark this: Unless you accept God's kingdom in the simplicity of a child, you'll never get in."* (Luke 18:15-17)

Here Jesus stopped to bless the children and then talked about our need to emulate the simplicity of children in their acceptance of God's kingdom.

If we want to impact others for Christ, we will invite women to accompany us when we teach a Bible study or go to a retreat. It's important to let women get close enough to see how we juggle our ministry lives and our personal lives. Perhaps we'll invite them to go grocery shopping, or to a concert with us, or to join our family at the zoo for a day. Married or single, we can invite women to our homes so they can feel invited into our lives and observe how we interact with our spouses and children or roommates.

I invited a younger speaker to join me at a recent out-of-town ministry trip. When her note of thanks came in the mail, the content wasn't directed toward my gifts of evangelism, exhortation, or teaching. She wrote, "I loved eavesdropping as you talked to your husband on the phone (while we were at the hotel). You were so obviously interested in him and his day. Your mutual respect and love for each other impressed me and convicted me to be a more active listener and encourager of my husband."

When we invite people to be involved in our lives, we often don't realize they are learning as much by what they observe in our interaction with our families and coworkers as they do from our carefully prepared instruction.

Jesus' "Walk And Talk" Was a Powerful Witnessing Tool

Late one night Nicodemus, a Pharisee and prominent leader among the Jews, visited Jesus and said:

> "Rabbi, we all know you're a teacher straight from God. No one could do all the God-pointing, God-revealing acts you do if God weren't in on it."
>
> Jesus said, "You're absolutely right. Take it from me: Unless a person is born from above, it's not possible to see what I'm pointing to—to God's kingdom."
>
> "How can anyone," asked Nicodemus, "be born who has already been born and grown up? You can't re-enter your mother's womb and be born again. What are you saying with this 'born-from-above' talk?"
>
> Jesus said, "You're not listening. Let me say it again. . . . The person who takes shape within is formed by something you can't see and touch—the Spirit—and becomes a living spirit."
>
> Jesus said, "You're a respected teacher of Israel and you don't know these basics? Listen carefully. I'm speaking sober truth to you. . . . This is how much God loved the world: He gave His Son, his one and only Son. And this

is why: so that no one need be destroyed; by believing in him, anyone can have a whole and lasting life. God didn't go to all the trouble of sending his Son merely to point an accusing finger, telling the world how bad it was. . . . Anyone who trusts in him is acquitted." (John 3:1-18)

An astonishing thought hit me as I reread this story. *The gospel message was delivered from the mouth of the Savior — and Nicodemus didn't accept it* (as far as we're told). Perhaps Jesus wanted us to realize that "walking the talk" and communicating the truth of the gospel message is an essential part of being a Christian — whether or not the individual responds positively. Our mission is to use the opportunities given to us to communicate truth when we are given those opportunities.

Deborah Henry left her job at an investment research firm in New York City. She was tired of working for an authoritarian boss who barked commands at her and didn't have "please" and "thank you" in his vocabulary. When she took a new job as assistant to a prolific Christian author, she expected the same brash and disrespectful treatment. After all, he was a *man* with power and authority over her!

However, during her first year as his assistant, she noticed a gentleness in his tone of voice, even when he was under enormous pressure. He was firm but didn't repay injury with injury. He seemed unconcerned about taking credit, yet gave it freely and undeservedly to people who needed to have it — including her!

Unlike her previous employer, he treated her as kindly as he treated his highly impressive professional friends and associates. He valued her comments and complimented her work. She began to feel a purpose and significance in the order of her days.

Deborah became curious about the way he handled his life, compared with the way she handled her own life. Working with this man was like breathing fresh air for the first time, and she sensed from his marriage, his work relationships, and his children that life could be different. She states, "He was the first man who treated me with unconditional respect, not because I deserved his respect, but because he treated everyone he met with respect. The doorman in the elevator received the same smile that the President of the United States did."

Deborah's curiosity grew as her boss instilled in her a sense of worth that made her willing to dare to search for deeper meaning in her obscure existence. She said, "Often, when I scratched the surface of my soul, I found nothing. . . . I can still remember the emptiness."

One day her employer asked for her opinion about a line in a book he was writing. "What do you think of this line?" he asked. The line described the main character's search for the meaning of life.

Deborah immediately said, "I think it should say he was trying to find his *center*."

"I like that." he said. "That's very good . . . finding one's center. Very nicely put."

As Deborah looked at her kind employer, she knew that he understood what it meant to be *centered*. She visualized her own center as a deep, dark well. She blurted out, "I yearn for wholeness, too. . . . Something big is missing. I've been going to church on my lunch break . . . looking for a home. Do you go to church?"

That day a busy man took the time to share his faith with Deborah, a struggling employee who was hungry for God. Soon after this meaningful conversation, Deborah found her *center* in Jesus Christ.

Deborah's employer demonstrated such Christlike characteristics through his daily "walking and talking" that she longed for a personal relationship with the Savior. Like Christ, this man's daily lifestyle was his strongest witnessing tool.

WHAT THE MASTER SAID ABOUT OUR WALK AND TALK

Most of us feel inadequate and a bit intimidated when we realize God might be able to use us to influence others positively through the way we live out our faith. Jesus gave us some specific teaching on the importance of our walk and our talk. The following are some of the main points He makes in the Sermon on the Mount.

BE "SALT-SEASONING"

"Let me tell you why you are here. You're here to be salt-seasoning that brings out the God-flavors of this earth. If you lose your saltiness, how will people taste godliness? You've lost your usefulness and will end up in the garbage" (Matthew 5:12).

Salt enhances flavor and also acts as a preservative. We become salt through bringing the essence of Jesus into everyday conversation. We influence others by being Christ to them. When we walk and talk what Scripture teaches, we will be salt in this world.

Patsy was a single, Christian, first grade teacher working in a public elementary school in Fremont, Michigan. One of her students was David, the son of a corporate pilot. David's parents, Bud and Jeannie, were impressed with the personal encouragement and academic assistance Patsy had provided for David. They wanted to get to know her better.

One day when Jeannie was picking up her son at school she said, "Patsy, our family is going up to Caberfae for a ski trip this weekend. Would you like to join us? It would be our way of thanking you for making such a big difference in David's life this year. Please come."

Patsy joined them for the weekend, and a friendship developed. Soon after the ski trip, Bud and Jeannie came to church with Patsy. They were intrigued with the intense spiritual commitment they observed in their son's young school teacher. It wasn't too much later when Patsy, in response to their questions about her life choices, told them of her personal faith in Christ. Within a short time, both Bud and Jeannie professed faith in Christ — and it all began when a first-grade teacher practiced what it means to be "salt-seasoning" in the life of her students — and in the lives of their parents.

Being salt-seasoning does not mean preaching at people or browbeating them with our list of what's right and wrong. It doesn't mean carrying a ten-pound Bible on top of our grocery cart or being obnoxious with the verbalization of our faith. It *does* mean living out the task God gave us to do today the way a Christ-follower should. Patsy lived like a Christian — in and out of her classroom. Her confidence, love, and genuine compassion for one of her students eventually opened the door for her to respond to the genuine questions his parents had about what it means to become a Christian.

GO PUBLIC WITH YOUR FAITH

Jesus said, "You're here to be light, bringing out the God-colors in the world. God is not a secret to be kept. We're going public with this, as public as a city on a hill. If I make you light-bearers, you don't think I'm going to hide you under a bucket, do you? I'm putting you on a

light stand. Now that I've put you there on a hilltop, on a light stand —
shine!" (Matthew 5:14-16).

As Christian women, we should be a light to people within our own
sphere of influence. Cathy Gallagher, a former marketing manager for a
medium-sized company, wrote to tell me about a woman who worked
as a receptionist in her office. She described Dawn Patterson as a wife
and mother of four sons and two stepsons whose commitment to Christ
shows in her eyes, her words, and her actions. Every morning Dawn
sends what she calls "The E-Mail Daily Bread" to fellow Christian
employees who need spiritual encouragement. Cathy said:

> My drive to work can be unsettling and I arrive at the
> office to the sound of phones ringing and people lined
> up at the door of the office waiting to discuss issues and
> business challenges. Even if I read Scripture first thing in
> the morning, it's hard to keep that peaceful feeling all day.
> The first day I received Dawn's unique e-mail was the day
> after I noticed her studying her Bible in the lunchroom
> during her break. I stopped to chat briefly with her and
> she found out I was a Christian. She never once men-
> tioned her "e-mail ministry," but the next day I received
> my first copy of this devotional.
>
> She sends it first thing in the morning to about
> twenty-five employees in our company and adds people
> to the list whenever she discovers they are Christians. She
> sends it quietly—no fanfare—and she expects nothing
> back from any of us who receive it. I love knowing that
> my serving of "Daily Bread" will be waiting for me, to

read and absorb any time of the day I need a spiritual boost. I find it comforting to see the list of my colleagues who also love the Lord at the top of the e-mail message. One hundred people work for our company and I believe our next step is for the Christians in this building to learn how to work together to have an even greater influence on each other and on our colleagues who haven't yet committed to the Lord.

As Jesus-followers, we need to take every opportunity to demonstrate our faith. Our mandate is to walk and talk like Christians, being a visible beacon of light in a world of darkness. Dawn is a courageous woman of faith who is *intentionally* influencing the Christians in her company. But the *unintentional* part of her influence is that she has helped the believers in her office complex to identify each other — and it may give them the momentum to cultivate impact moments with the unbelievers in the office.

LET PEOPLE "HANG OUT" WITH YOU

Jesus taught, "Keep open house; be generous with your lives. By opening up to others, you'll prompt people to open up with God, this generous Father in heaven" (Matthew 5:16).

In an interview with *Christianity Today* magazine, Esther Burroughs, Southern Baptist author and speaker, expressed concern about the separation of families and the lack of contact between generations.

We no longer have the luxury of being raised by an extended family. . . . The Lord is looking for women to get

out of the church and into the world for ministry. . . . [I]
hope to encourage women to become all that God wants
them to be. . . . Generation X is looking for an authen-
tic, live, show-me, love-me, walk-with-me, and guide-
me person. . . . Some women in their twenties who visit
church have no clue where or how to buy a Bible. But
they want to know because they see peers underlining or
highlighting words of Scripture.[2]

Barb McPhail was one of those new Christians who needed that
kind of help. She says, "When I welcomed Christ into my life as Lord
and Savior, I was a twenty-four-year-old party girl." She explains, "My
prayer of repentance was, 'Goodbye Schuberg's Bar. Goodbye party
buddies. Hello Jesus!'"

She found herself longing for a friend and mentor who would help
her get to know Christ better. Within a few short months God replaced
her former party friends with the love and support of a thirty-three-
year-old wife and mother who loved God. She said, "From the first
moment I met Lee, it was as if God knit our hearts together."

Lee not only let Barb "hang out" with her, she instructed her in
biblical truth and in matters of practical Christian living. Barb describes
their relationship in the following way:

In the sixteen years since we met, Lee has been my
mother, sister, best friend, prayer partner, and adviser.
Like an empty sponge, I eagerly soaked up all the love and
insight about God's kingdom she had to offer. She never
professed to have all the answers, but she was quick to

say, "Let's pray." To this day, whenever I hear those words,
I'm reminded that God fulfilled the desire of my heart for
a friend and mentor through Lee.

When we allow a younger woman to spend time with us daily (not just during special appointments, Bible studies, and lunch dates), we give her a chance to see how a Christian should live her life. She may at times see examples of when we blow it with our husbands, roommates, children, or friends, but it's an honest view of life.

Jesus knew that by opening our homes and our hearts to people, they could learn how to be open with God. By being generous with our lives, our homes, and our background knowledge of God and His Word, we provide the soil in which young Christian women can become mature Christ-followers who will also have an impact on others.

"WALK YOUR TALK" AND "TALK YOUR WALK"

Matthew 5:48 says, "*Grow up.* You're kingdom subjects. Now live like it. Live out your God-created identity. Live generously and graciously toward others, the way God lives toward you." Jesus was saying "walk your talk" and "talk your walk." If you are a believer, live for Christ in every aspect of your life, being careful to bless others in the way God has blessed you.

Susan Hunt, in a book titled *Spiritual Mothering*, tells the story of Miss Elizabeth, a woman who definitely lived out her God-created identity and impacted many women:

> *Mrs. Elizabeth Scott, known affectionately as "Miss"*
> *Elizabeth, was 76. She was a quiet, humble woman*

who did not have a high-profile ministry, yet the church was packed for her funeral. The hundreds of people who attended were deeply moved by her death. I was particularly struck by my conversations with the women. I thought that Miss Elizabeth was my special encourager — my personal fan club — my cheerleader. Since knowing her, I have had more confidence to assume responsibilities because I knew she was in my corner praying and cheering me on. What astounded me was that it seemed as if every woman there had the same relationship with her! She had done for them what she had done for me — yet it had been done in such a quiet way that we each thought we were her special project.

I simply could not believe the women who talked about their families being invited to a meal in her home, or those who told how she had invited them to our church, or how she had been the first person to greet them when they visited the church, or the women who talked about receiving cards and telephone calls from her.

As I have contemplated the power of her life, I have also been struck with what she did not do. Gossip, complaint, and criticism had no part in her life.

Miss Elizabeth loved the young women in the church. . . . What she was and what she did, any Christian woman can be and do. She had no extraordinary gifts or circumstances. She simply loved Jesus and lived each day for His glory. She imitated Him by serving those around her.[3]

Becoming a woman of influence is simply a matter of loving Jesus and obeying His teachings on how we "walk" and "talk" every day of our lives.

PRACTICAL WAYS TO IMPLEMENT JESUS' TEACHING

If we believe spiritual development is an essential part of a person's journey toward maturity, we need to be Christian women who are willing to take the following action steps:

Recognize the need. With the fragmented families and transience in our society, young moms often live across the country from biological relatives who could provide answers to basic questions about life and faith. There are many more women who long to be mentored than women available, willing, and enthusiastic about meeting that need. If Christ has changed your life and you believe the Bible has the answers to today's problems, there's someone younger who needs to hear you verbalize how you walk with Jesus on a daily basis.

Accentuate your strengths and minimize your liabilities. Impacting lives as Jesus did doesn't require perfection. It requires the availability of a more spiritually mature woman who is willing to walk beside a younger woman and be a friend. Too many women feel they can't be a positive influence if they have not "arrived" spiritually. But the best mentor is one who admits failure and allows a younger woman to watch her deal with the effects of failure (or sin) and learn from the process. The only perfect mentor who ever lived was Jesus. If you are waiting for that level of perfection before you make yourself available, it won't happen.

Continue to grow spiritually yourself. The best mentor is someone who walks and talks with Jesus every day. Your Christian life becomes a natural rhythm of assimilating God's Word into your heart and life and translating what you learn into practical daily living. Author and speaker Kathy Peel says:

> God's Word acts like a time-release vitamin. For example, I had toast and coffee for breakfast this morning. I don't feel it running through my system right now, but it is. It's the same way when we read God's Word. When we put it into our mind, we don't feel it working. But all of a sudden, one day we realize we have the ability to overcome a temptation or the answer to a problem.[4]

That's what "the principle of walking and talking" is all about. When a younger woman hears us giving biblical solutions to problems or when we talk about a recent temptation and how we responded, it gets us off a pedestal and she can ask honest questions and admit her own failings without fear of rejection.

Invest your time in a younger woman. It is never easy to add an "unpaid" job to your life. It means the sacrifice of time. I have met a few women who don't want to be bothered. There is sometimes an attitude of "I raised my kids, I served my time in the church kitchen and in the nursery, I taught Sunday school for years, and now I'm retired. I paid my dues and I'm headed for the golf course." However, a woman with Christ's heart says, "God has taught me so much and my greatest joy would be to help someone avoid some of the mistakes I made and give her encouragement when life gets hard."

When we consciously invest our lives in younger women and tell them we're available to respond to their questions day or night, something exciting happens to *us*. We realize our lives have more purpose, more significance, and more meaning than we ever dreamed we would experience. When we impact the lives of others *on purpose*, we celebrate their personal growth, their emerging spiritual maturity, and their growing confidence — and we humbly realize God allowed us the unique privilege of being part of the process. And then we have to tell somebody else they need to try it, too!

Speaker, author, and radio host Pam Farrel says,

> *Your infectiousness will spread when you are flexible and tenacious in seeking to be an influence. Infectious women have a "can-do" attitude. . . . Every Christian woman is to be a woman of influence. Every woman is to make disciples. Every woman is to go into the world and make a difference for Jesus. . . . Don't wait for women to ask you to mentor them; challenge women to be mentored. Don't wait for a woman to challenge you to be mentored; ask her to mentor you. Don't wait until women in the world ask you for help; offer it ahead of time. Don't wait until they ask about Jesus, go tell them.*[5]

Let's live in such a way that our "walk" and our "talk" enable us to be women of influence. Let's initiate relationships that will give hope, help, and encouragement to others. Let's be *infectious*. Let's be "on purpose" Christian women who realize every encounter we have has the potential of becoming an impact moment for the person who crosses our path today.

Chapter Five

THE PRINCIPLE OF STORYTELLING

Few things touch us as deeply as a good story. God knows this about us. That is why I believe so much of Scripture is written as narrative. God knows that He can get through to us when we see, hear, and experience His story.[1]

—MAX MCLEAN

MY HEART ACHED AS I saw the disappointment etched on my son's furrowed brow. Every day after school he rushed in the back door to the kitchen counter to see if he'd received a letter of appointment to the United States Naval Academy. Graduation was just two months away, and he still had not heard anything.

For two and a half years J.P. had focused on this goal. He had gone to a Christian leadership camp the summer after his sophomore year and came back knowing that one man could change the world, and he wanted to be that man. "Mom and Dad, I've made some major decisions while I've been away. I want to lead our nation back to God, to correct the wrongs and make Him first in everything. . . . I believe the place where I can get the best education for this purpose is at the U.S. Naval Academy."

We finally called the admissions office and learned that, although J.P. was well-qualified, there were over twelve thousand candidates for approximately one thousand appointments — and J.P. had not been selected. It was the death of a dream.

Later that month, I was speaking at a mountain retreat in Southern California. One night I sat at a table in the dining room with a group of winsome women. One of them turned to me and said, "Carol, tell us about your family. How can we pray for you?" Her tone was sincere and the women seemed genuinely interested, so I told them about J.P.'s disappointing news. "My son has been so convinced that he was to go to the Naval Academy I'm afraid we're facing his first experience of being deeply disappointed in God. He thought God was leading him there, but the door is closing. Will you pray for God's will to be accomplished, and for J.P. to accept whatever God has for his future?" They said they would.

Six weeks went by. J.P. went through the formalities of high school graduation and made plans to accept a scholarship to an engineering school, but his heart wasn't in it.

The week after graduation, he began working on a construction team for a builder in the area. A few days after he started the job, I left home early to run errands. As I returned and came through the front door, the phone was ringing. I said, "Hello," and the voice on the other end of the line said, "May I please speak to Jason Kent?" I explained he was working on a construction site all day and was not reachable by phone, but I told the caller I'd be happy to take a message.

The official sounding voice continued, "I'm calling from the admissions office at the Naval Academy. We have a meeting scheduled tomorrow morning to decide on an appointment and I need to know if Jason was offered a position at the Academy at this late date, would he still accept?"

I was incredulous. "Would he accept? He'd be on the next plane to the East Coast!" Then I paused and added, "My son is so interested in coming to Annapolis that I'm hesitant to put him through this level of disappointment twice. Are you telling me that you have ten good candidates and you'll be selecting *one* of them tomorrow morning, or are you telling me my son has a very good chance of receiving an appointment?"

She responded, "Please hold."

I was hyperventilating by this time, but gained control as she returned to the phone. She continued, "I'm not really authorized to say this, but your son has a very good chance of receiving an appointment tomorrow morning." After assuring her once again that he would *definitely* accept the appointment, I hung up.

I glanced at the answering machine and noticed the message light was blinking. As I pressed the button, I heard: "Carol, you may not remember me, but I attended the retreat you spoke at in Southern California last April. Several of us sat around a table in the dining room and you told us about what your son was going through regarding his disappointment about not getting the appointment to the Naval Academy. Every day since our meeting I have been praying for Jason regarding this situation. I've been praying for God's will to be done in the whole matter and that He would work mightily in Jason's heart through this experience, regardless of what the end result is. This morning I felt especially prompted to pray for him. I just thought I'd call to find out what has happened. I won't leave my number. I'll just call back another time. Goodbye."

Fighting back tears, I listened to the message again. When I came to the spot where she said, "and this morning I felt especially prompted to pray," I could hold the tears back no longer. At the very moment she was praying for Jason, there was a meeting in the admissions office in Annapolis, Maryland, and his name was selected as one of the next potential appointees.

Jason returned home just before dinner. He already knew that his name would be approved for an appointment at the Academy the following morning because Gene and I had driven out to the work site earlier in the day to give him the good news. As he entered the house, I said, "J. P., there's a message on the answering machine you need to hear."

He listened to that recording at least six times. He had tears in his eyes as he put his arms around me. "Mom," he said, "if I had gotten into the Academy early or if I'd gotten in easily, I would have thought it was because *I* was good enough or *I* was smart enough, but the way this appointment came, I know that, through prayer, God opened a door where there was no door."

That evening I picked up my Bible and read some familiar Scriptures:

> *The prayer of a person living right with God is something powerful to be reckoned with. (James 5:16)*

> *Don't fret or worry. Instead of worrying, pray. Let petitions and praises shape your worries into prayers, letting God know your concerns. Before you know it, a sense of God's wholeness, everything coming together for good, will come and settle you down. It's wonderful what happens when Christ displaces worry at the center of your life. (Philippians 4:6-7)*

My anxiety over my son's disappointment had been acute. I often had chosen worry over prayer during those months of anxious waiting. But God put a powerful intercessor in our lives. I believe her prayers helped to open a closed door. News of the official appointment came the next day. It was an experience that will forever remind us of the importance of choosing prayer over worry.

Making Spiritual Truth Relevant

After reading this story, you have learned some specific things about me. You know I'm a mother who worried about her son during a major transition point in his life. You know I wrestle with anxiety much like you do. I hope you know that I have found God's Word to be comforting and true. And you know I believe God answers prayer. I could have told you facts about my family and quoted Bible verses about prayer. But because I wrapped the verses in a personal story, you will remember the main application longer.

Stories intrigue us and keep us guessing about the outcomes and responses. They fill us with anticipation. They also can answer our questions. Stories can teach complex theological truths in ways that do not intimidate or threaten.

Stories connect us to the storyteller, providing companionship and comfort. What parent hasn't heard a child say, "Please read me another story," or, "Please read that story *again*." Sometimes the benefit of the story is more in the warmth of human connection than in the message of the story itself.

Garrison Keillor begins his weekly monologue on his public radio program, *A Prairie Home Companion*, with these words: "It's been a quiet week in Lake Wobegon, my home town. . . ." Keillor's storytelling ability has attracted national attention. I recently listened to his program while driving in my car. Most of his stories describe everyday life and ordinary people in a very homespun way. It wasn't *what* he said that kept me listening, it was the *way* he said it. I felt like he was talking to me personally.

Storytelling isn't new. It's one of the oldest forms of entertainment and communication. However, today this wonderful technique is being rediscovered. Max McLean, founder of the Fellowship for the Performing Arts, is one of the foremost Christian storytellers in the country. He was asked a series of questions by the staff of Leadership Network, and his answers are instructive.

LEADERSHIP: *What is the significance of storytelling in the culture in which we are now living?*

McLEAN: *I don't think storytelling has changed in terms of its impact because stories are the basic medium of all moral communication. Hollywood knows this; the TV industry knows this. The question is, What is the quality of the story you are telling? Does it have the force to stir the blood? That's why the Bible is the only book that "glows in the dark" because it has those stories . . . I am amazed at the communicators that have never quite understood that a story is not a story until it has been received. It is in the receiving that there is a combustion . . . it's a circuit that comes back to you — and that is communication. People today are saying, "Unless it touches me viscerally, existentially, experientially, I don't care. It may be as true as one plus one equals two, but it is meaningless to me." Now for good or ill, there are problems with that, but it is reality. There is an expectation that information has to do something . . . you can't just give it to me flat . . . it's got to have color . . . something underneath it.*

LEADERSHIP: *What advice would you give to people who are trying to communicate Truth in this age?*

McLean: *If the story does not touch you, doesn't get a rise out of you, it's not going to get a rise out of anyone else. Passion communicates. The key is that the story resonates . . . and you are thinking about it after you leave . . . and the next day you are thinking about it . . . that means it is permeating the culture.[2]*

George Barna agrees and adds further insight about communicating in today's culture:

Educational psychologists tell us that today's young people are "mosaic thinkers," able to put information together in new patterns, often arriving at unusual, novel, or surprising conclusions. This is in contrast to Boomers, Builders, and Seniors who are "linear thinkers," assembling facts in a predictable path and generally arriving at predictable conclusions. . . . Stories, to the postmodernist, relativistic mind, are undeniable: Experience is permitted where theology or philosophy is rejected.[3]

People are changing in the way they are willing (and able) to receive information. If truth is not wrapped in a package that causes us to *see, feel, hear,* and *taste* what's happening, the average person won't tune in long enough to listen. In other words, if we want to make a lasting impact on our culture, we need to become storytellers. We need to give life to the biblical points we are making by bringing color, emotion, and drama to our illustrations.

I became aware of the importance of stories as a young public speaker.

Young women who were in my audiences wrote letters in response to the messages they heard. Almost without fail, they would comment on a key illustration I had told and how it had changed their lives. When I told a story about being called "Big Lips" in the fourth grade by a boy I had a crush on, women identified with my loss of self-esteem. They identified with my spiritual failure when I told how, on a day I'd reserved for Bible study and prayer, I suddenly craved chocolate and went out of my way to purchase and then consume a sixteen-ounce Hershey bar, a huge Cadbury Caramello, and a giant-sized package of M&Ms. I ate so much I became ill and couldn't study. I soon realized women weren't remembering my outline, they were remembering my stories and their applications. Clearly, the Holy Spirit uses stories to change lives.

The Bible says, "[Jesus] taught by using stories, many stories" (Mark 4:2). As our culture changes and we understand more about postmodernism, we realize the importance of what Jesus modeled.

LEARNING FROM THE MASTER

Jesus was a master storyteller. He communicated spiritual truth through parables and word pictures. As He walked from city to town, He often used a common object — a loaf of bread, a stone, a lost coin, or types of soil — to make a spiritual application. As a result, His audience had an emotional connection with Him and with the point He was making.

Jim Lyon, pastor and host of a radio program called "ViewPoint," explains: "Identification with the audience (establishing common ground) is the first principle of all effective communication. In this Jesus is the stellar model. He excelled at transforming the ordinary icons and emblems of His secular culture into illustrations of spiritual truth."[4]

JESUS USED ORDINARY OBJECTS TO COMMUNICATE SPIRITUAL TRUTHS

Jesus often taught profound truths by helping people to visualize what He was talking about. "[He] routinely built bridges to His audience to help people see the world from Heaven's view."[5]

Here are just a few examples of how He used a familiar object to illustrate a greater truth.

> *"God's kingdom is* like a pine nut *that a farmer plants. It is quite small as seeds go, but in the course of years it grows into a huge pine tree, and eagles build nests in it." (Matthew 13:31, emphasis added)*

> *"God's kingdom is* like yeast *that a woman works into the dough for dozens of loaves of barley bread—and waits while the dough rises." (Matthew 13:33, emphasis added)*

Many of Jesus' parables also were developed around ordinary objects or situations. For example, the parable of the lost coin:

> *"Or imagine a woman who has ten coins and loses one. Won't she light a lamp and scour the house, looking in every nook and cranny until she finds it? And when she finds it you can be sure she'll call her friends and neighbors: 'Celebrate with me! I found my lost coin!' Count on it — that's the kind of party God's angels throw every time one lost soul turns to God." (Luke 15:8-10)*

Jesus told this story so His listeners would understand that every lost person is important to the Father. Even if one individual in a group is outside His fold, it's a major issue to Him — and it should be to us, too. He emphasizes this point by helping us to envision an angelic celebration when one person begins a walk of faith. The mental image of angels throwing a party brings emotion, color, and excitement to our understanding of the value of one person coming to Christ. Jesus connects with His listeners by painting a picture that evokes an emotional response.

As women who want to make a lasting impact on others, we need to find "points of identification" that will help women understand and apply what we are teaching them. You and I may not be able to tell parables in the same way Jesus did, but we can help others visualize our message.

Sometimes I use objects as springboards into a story or point.

- Holding up a tea kettle, I may say, "Have you ever felt like you've been in hot water up to your neck? I was in a situation like that this week. . . ."
- With a pancake turner in my hand, I ask, "Do you ever feel like you need to be scraped off the ceiling? When I was in my early thirties, I miscarried a child we wanted very much. . . ."
- Carrying my laundry basket, I might say, "I was a basket case the first year of my son's life. I was sure no one could take care of him as well as I could. I was convinced if I left him in the church nursery, he would get a cold. . . ."

I'm sure you've figured out that if we did this all the time, it would get a little hokey and wouldn't be effective. Good teachers use variety. Train your brain to see potential illustrations that will help to make truth memorable to others. Whether you are creating a mental image through a powerful illustration or using a concrete object as a springboard for teaching truth, people will remember the point longer if you help them visualize it.

JESUS TAUGHT THAT STORIES CAN MAKE PEOPLE RECEPTIVE TO SPIRITUAL TRUTH

Jesus told the disciples: "You've been given insight into God's kingdom — you know how it works. But to those who can't see it yet, everything comes in stories, creating readiness, nudging them toward receptive insight" (Mark 4:11). In other words, stories capture the imagination of skeptical people and warm them up, first to the storyteller, and then to the message of the story.

This is still true today. Jay and Melanie Stewart moved into a new subdivision and immediately tried to establish a friendly relationship with their neighbors. Their real purpose was to reach their neighbors with the gospel.

Mike and Michelle lived two doors away. Jay and Melanie often waved at them and there was an occasional "hello" at the neighborhood pool, but their attempts to build a relationship seemed to be met with a cold response. Jay invited Mike over for a pickup basketball game and sent an invitation with a personal note for their church's Easter production. Nothing. Each time he saw them, Jay prayed, "Father, please open some door; help me to seize an opportunity to talk with Mike and Michelle. Touch their hearts and draw them to you." Three years went by.

Early one Sunday morning Jay opened the front door and let Stormie, their cocker spaniel, out for her "business" walk. Minutes later Jay opened the door to let Stormie in, and as Stormie raced into the house, he was accompanied by one of the most appalling and deplorable smells he had ever inhaled. Stormie had taken a direct hit from a skunk. The weeks that followed were exhausting — countless bathings with tomato juice, lemon juice, special skunk deodorizer, and dog shampoo.

Late one afternoon as Jay was working in his yard, the Spirit of God prompted his heart with this thought: "Go now and tell Mike the story of all you've been through with the skunk." The thought seemed humorous and absurd. Jay built his case: "God, that's ridiculous. What will I say to him about a skunk? He already thinks I'm strange. I just can't do that." But the thought intensified and he headed to Mike's house with the visual aid for his story — Stormie, the "skunky" cocker spaniel — not far behind.

Jay relayed the story and told Mike he might need to keep a close eye on *his* dog as some other neighbors had experienced similar problems with skunks. "Thanks," Mike said. "I'm a little out of touch with what is going on in the neighborhood. I've been at the hospital for the past seven days with Michelle. She has had some problems with her pregnancy and needed surgery."

Jay and Melanie made meals for the family and Melanie visited regularly to check on Michelle. Several weeks later, Michelle went into labor and delivered a healthy baby girl eight weeks early. Jay went to the hospital several times and prayed with Mike and Michelle. Finally the day arrived when they could take Baby Maggie home from the hospital. Jay and Melanie brought them a gift, and with tears in his eyes, Mike thanked them for the numerous ways they had helped them through their crisis.

"We're gonna come to your church soon, too," he said. And they did. On Easter Sunday they came — and they've been there ever since! A skunk story paved the way for neighborhood evangelism.

JESUS TOLD STORIES IN INFORMAL SETTINGS

Mark 4:1 records, "He went back to teaching by the sea. A crowd built up to such a great size that he had to get into an offshore boat, using the boat as a pulpit as the people pushed to the water's edge." If we want to follow Jesus' example, we need to be open to impacting lives in a non-church setting.

During my early years of ministry with teenagers, I usually didn't have a formal lectern. Most of the time I shared illustrations in a casual, natural way from a hayloft, a school desk, a bench at a roller rink, or while riding to an event on a church bus. Young people crowded in and I told stories of what God had been doing in my life through other people.

In *The Second Coming of the Church*, George Barna says:

> *Their [mosaic thinkers'] diet of mass media, combined with the uncritical embrace of computer technologies and the national shift in morals and values, has resulted in an entirely new filter through which Americans receive and interpret information. . . . The emergence of the new filter mandates a new style of sermon or lesson development and delivery. . . . Presenters who address the audience without constant reference to notes, and those who do not "hide" behind a pulpit, also seem to generate a more positive response from their listeners.*[6]

In other words, young women today will not be affected as powerfully by a well-rehearsed, polished speaker who stands at a stiff microphone behind a shiny lectern. They'll listen more closely if we share biblical truth through our informal stories of how Christ has changed our lives.

When you tell your own testimony, just be yourself. You don't need fancy language or a course in communications. Just tell what your life was like before coming to know Christ and what the difference is since you've grown in your walk with Him. If you became a Christian at a young age, you can talk about what Jesus means to you and why you love Him. Try inviting a neighbor over for coffee or a coworker to lunch. Get to know her, and look for opportunities to tell your story. Don't worry if you get emotional. Genuine tears often touch hearts more deeply than the most polished presentations.

JESUS ALMOST ALWAYS MADE THE APPLICATION CLEAR WHEN HE TOLD A STORY

In Mark 4, Jesus relates the story of the farmer who plants seed. Some of the seed is scattered on the road where the birds eat it. Some of it falls in the gravel and sprouts quickly, but withers when the sun comes up because it didn't put down roots. Other seed fell in the weeds and was strangled by those weeds. He ends this part of the story by saying, "Some fell on good earth and came up with a flourish, producing a harvest exceeding his wildest dreams" (Mark 4:8).

When Jesus finished telling the story of the scattered seed, He turned to the disciples and said, "Do you see how this story works? All my stories work this way" (verse 13). Jesus then clarified His point: The way people respond to God's Word is just like what happened in the story. Some people are like the seed that falls on the road and Satan snatches it away. Some are like the seed that lands in the gravel: There's quick, enthusiastic response, but such shallow character that when emotions wear off and troubles come, there's nothing left. Others are like the seed that falls in the weeds and are overcome with worries. He ends by describing the seed planted in good earth that produces a harvest beyond description (loosely paraphrased from Mark 4:14-20).

When I tell a story when I'm speaking, I often write out the application because it helps me be sure the meaning is clear and concise. Even though I don't read the application when I'm speaking, I am much less wordy when I've gone to the work of writing it out. This process gives me confidence in the point I'm making.

LET PEOPLE TELL THEIR OWN STORIES

As women who want to impact our culture, we need to be alert and *look* for opportunities to illustrate truth through stories, personal illustrations, and object lessons.

We also need to encourage and help others tell stories — beginning with their own story. Every Christian has a story to tell: "Anyone united with the Messiah gets a fresh start, is created new. The old life is gone; a new life burgeons!" (2 Corinthians 5:17).

Jill Briscoe tells of being in Eastern Europe ministering to a group of Bulgarian women who had been out from under the Communist regime for only eight years. The spiritual needs were great and many women were responding to the gospel. Jill's interpreter was a young woman named Gabriela, whom she describes as "typical of the new generation of Jesus pleasers." Jill explained:

> She translated my messages with fire, accuracy, and brilliance. I was going to teach on 1 Kings 17, about the widow at Zarephath.

"I lost my firstborn son, my only child, too," Gabriela explained. *"Just like the widow in the story."*

"Gabriela," I said, *"When I get to that part of the message, would you like to share your experience of God's help?"*

"It is two years since it happened, and I have not yet spoken of this," she replied.

"Maybe God wants you to do it today," I suggested. *"But if you don't want to, just tell me when the time comes."*

As I approached that point in the message, I paused and turned to look at her. She was wide-eyed and luminous as she began to tell her moving story. Now the passion in her words was mixed with the gentle rain of her tears. Gabriela spoke of "the valley of the shadow of death," and explained how she discovered that for the Christian, who is called to walk in that dreaded valley, where there's a shadow, there's also a light.

The Spirit of God took over the meeting and I stepped back, giving her space. Of course, I could not understand a word she was saying, but there was no mistaking the Spirit and the power with which she spoke. She became, in that anointed moment, the speaker of the day — *our teacher and instructor in righteousness, a sweet child pointing us to her Jesus, a child full of the Holy Ghost. When it was over, I closed the meeting and gathered up my notes. They would be used another day.*[7]

When we provide opportunities for younger Christians to tell their stories of God's transforming power and love, we create powerful experiences that may change the direction of their lives and powerfully influence the lives of those who listen.

TELL THE GRAND STORY

Lael Arrington, a speaker, professor of cultural issues, and author of *Worldproofing Your Kids,* is quick to point out the problem with our postmodern world. In a lecture titled "Thoroughly Postmodern Millie and Willie," she said:

> *In the Middle Ages and in the Modern Age, life was perceived as a story with a beginning, an end, a plot, and characters. People visualized themselves playing a part in a larger story. However, the postmodern person has no sense of being part of a grand story. They see no author and no story. Each person lives in his or her own small story, trying to make it as interesting and enjoyable as possible.*[8]

As Christians, we *know* there is a grand story and Jesus continues to be the example of "the greatest story ever told." That motivates me to keep telling *His* story and to tell the story of how He's changed my life and has the power to change the lives of others.

Are you equipped and ready to tell your story? *There is a grand story,* and you and I have the awesome privilege of telling it again and again so those we touch can "live happily ever after" — with God in heaven!

Chapter Six

The Principle of Asking Questions

For a man who had all the answers, Jesus asked a lot of questions.[1]

— Candy Davison

ON A HOT MIDWESTERN AFTERNOON, reporters from several area newspapers swarmed over the competitors at a state track meet, interviewing the winner in a highly contested footrace. They wanted to know: How did you train? Is this your best event? What did it feel like to win?

Before long, only one reporter remained. Struggling to come up with an angle for his story, he asked the shy runner, "Is there anything you had to overcome in order to be here today?"

"Well, yes," said the track star. "As a child, I had polio."

The real story was uncovered by the right question.

Who would have thought that a single question could be so powerful? And yet, that is often the case. According to authors Robert and Pamela Crosby, "Good questions create interest; great ones inspire a response. Good questions open conversations; great ones open souls. Good questions raise issues; great ones evoke dreams and visions. Good questions elicit ideas; great questions uncover needs."[2]

Jesus asked questions that opened people's souls, uncovering long-held dreams and deep-seated needs.

LEARNING FROM THE MASTER

Everywhere Jesus went, He used questions to make His point or reinforce His teaching. Sometimes He used questions to bring conviction or reveal hypocrisy. His questions often made people think about who He was and why He came.

In *How to Ask Great Questions,* Karen Lee-Thorp observes:

> *Jesus' questions were simple, clear, never condescending, always provocative. They made people think for themselves and examine their hearts. Jesus' questions were always fresh and attuned to the unique needs of the people He was talking to. Instead of following a rote method, He seems to have thought about how His questions would affect His audience.*[3]

Let's take a closer look at the different ways in which Jesus used questions.

JESUS USED QUESTIONS TO EXPOSE FALSEHOOD AND REVEAL TRUTH

At times Jesus asked questions to reveal what was truly in people's hearts. This was especially true with the Pharisees, who represented themselves as people who loved and obeyed God but were, in reality, hypocrites. One example of this is seen in Matthew 21:23-27 (NIV).

Jesus entered the temple courts, and, while he was teaching, the chief priests and the elders of the people came to him. "By what authority are you doing these things?" they asked. "And who gave you this authority?"

Jesus replied, "I will also ask you one question. If you answer me, I will tell you by what authority I am doing these things. John's baptism — where did it come from? Was it from heaven, or from men?"

They discussed it among themselves and said, "If we say, 'From heaven,' he will ask, 'Then why didn't you believe him?' But if we say, 'From men' — we are afraid of the people, for they all hold that John was a prophet."

So they answered Jesus, "We don't know."

Then he said, "Neither will I tell you by what authority I am doing these things."

Jesus knew that the Pharisees weren't sincere when they asked Him by whose authority He performed miracles; He knew they wanted to accuse Him of blasphemy and were trying to trick Him. So He answered their question with another question, exposing what was really in their hearts.

Women of influence often have people who come to them for help. Many times the plea is sincere, but not always. Sometimes it is wise for us to ask questions that will expose whether or not the person truly wants 100 percent spiritual healing or whether she enjoys being needy.

Early in our marriage, when Gene and I were youth directors in our church, one sixteen-year-old named Char seemed bent on a path of destruction. She verbally put herself down. She got into alcohol and drug abuse, and she hung out with other teens who were making negative choices. With her mouth she told us that she wanted to live for God and make decisions that reflected a Christian lifestyle, but her behavior reflected another story.

I invited Char to our home while Gene was away, and during

a relaxing, nonthreatening visit, I asked her some of the following questions:

- *"Are the choices you are making right now making you happy?"* That was a given; she definitely wasn't happy.
- *"What benefits are you receiving from your current lifestyle?"* I urged her to be open about this and her answers were truthful — friends, acceptance, instant gratification, and so on.
- *"What do you want your life to be like five years from now?"* To a teenager, that's an eternity, but it did make her think about where her current choices might lead.
- *"Char, which do you love more: Jesus, or what you are doing to destroy your body and mind? It's your choice."* I had wept with her and prayed with her. Our relationship was close enough for me to be this confrontational. She cried with me as she answered that question.
- *"What can I do to help you? You've said you love Jesus more than your addiction to drugs and alcohol. Are you willing to follow through with getting professional help for these addictions? Could I be an accountability partner in your life?"*

My questions — combined with listening, love, and God's intervention — helped Char to see what dangerous ground she had been walking on. The next few months proved to be a difficult struggle for Char, but she made better choices and began to change her behavior.

JESUS' QUESTIONS EXPOSED PEOPLE'S DEEPEST LONGINGS

In chapter 2 we looked at an interesting encounter between Jesus and a blind beggar. The beggar must have heard stories about Jesus because when he heard who was passing by, he cried out, "Jesus, have mercy on me!" Scripture tells us that Jesus stopped and asked the man to be brought to Him, and His first words were a question: "What do you want me to do for you?" The man replied, "Lord, I want to see" (Luke 18:41, NIV).

What do you want me to do for you? This question is so powerful, it deserves mentioning again. When we are approached by a woman who wants to spend time with us, we need to ask her this same question. Does she want advice, a listening ear, to be discipled, a friend? Her answer can direct you in how you spend your time together, plus it can give you important information about how insightful and self-aware she might be.

Think back on this comment from Bobb Biehl quoted earlier in the book: "The single most teachable moment of any protégé's life is the few seconds immediately following a sincere question. No curriculum or checklist or theory could replace a mentor's life experience and compassion in such a teachable moment."[4] It's true. We need to listen closely to the answers women give to our key questions and then respond with our hearts, not just our heads.

Some of the questions I ask women to help them realize their deepest longings are:

- What are the five most important things in your life?
- What stress point are you experiencing that you would like to eliminate?
- What one thing would you like to change about your body?
- What one thing would you like to see change in your spiritual life?
- What were your expectations when you got married?
- What were your expectations when you had your first baby?

- In what area of your life do you need advice?
- What woman (historical or contemporary) would you most like to emulate?
- What did you want to grow up to do or to be? Have you fulfilled that dream?

Every time I ask one of these questions and the woman answers it honestly, we're drawn closer together. I try never to act shocked with the responses — even if I am. When longings are discussed, it's important to provide a safe place for honest answers.

JESUS' QUESTIONS TRIGGERED GROWTH IN FAITH

One of my favorite New Testament stories takes place after Jesus feeds the five thousand. Jesus insisted that the disciples get into a boat and go ahead of Him to Gennesaret. He climbed a mountain and spent time alone with God in prayer. A huge wind came up and the disciples were quaking with fear out in the middle of the lake. Jesus began walking to them on the water, but the disciples were convinced it was a ghost!

Jesus immediately brought a sense of calm to their faithless hearts: "Take courage! It is I. Don't be afraid" (Matthew 14:27, NIV).

Peter got excited and said, "Lord, if it's you . . . tell me to come to you on the water" (verse 28, NIV). Jesus invited Peter to come and he got out of the boat and began walking toward Jesus. But the wind was great and Peter's fear returned and he began to sink. He cried out, "Lord, save me!" (verse 30, NIV).

Jesus immediately reached out His hand, rescued Peter, and said, "You of little faith . . . why did you doubt?" (verse 31, NIV).

Todd Catteau, in an article titled "The Questions of Jesus"

comments:

> *Jesus . . . asked faith-building questions after episodes
> that demonstrated a lack of faith. In Matthew 14:31, for
> example, Jesus rescued Peter from his water-walk, then
> asked, "Why did you doubt?" That question had to ring
> in Peter's ears for the rest of his life and probably helped
> him through many other challenging situations.*[5]

You and I can do the same when working with people whose faith is going through tough times. During my assignment as director of the Alternative Education Program for Pregnant Teenagers, Tammy entered my life. She was a dynamic, attractive, energized high school senior with a 4.0 grade point average. She was captain of the cheerleading squad, but her life drastically changed when she got pregnant. She and Brad, the star quarterback of the football team, were in love, but they were both seventeen and, on the advice of their parents, they decided to wait to get married.

Tammy was devastated by what was happening in her life. She went from being one of the most popular girls in the senior class to leaving her school because of the pregnancy and coming to Alternative Ed to finish her classes so she could graduate. She was "pretty sure" of Brad's love, but she had seen him flirt with other girls and her confidence in their relationship was deteriorating.

I soon discovered that Tammy was a Christian. One day she blurted out, "I've wrecked my life. I've hurt my parents. I used to be pretty, but now I'm big and fat. I don't know if I can trust Brad to stay true to me. I'm just so afraid."

Putting my arm around her, I asked, "Tammy, what are you afraid of?"

She was most fearful of not having a husband and being a single mother with no future. I said, "Tammy, you told me you became a Christian just two years ago. Do you believe God will give you the strength to bring this baby into the world and to be a good mother—even if Brad isn't in your life?"

"Y-y-yes," she said.

I continued, "Do you know there's a verse in the Bible that says, 'Never will I leave you; never will I forsake you'?[6] What that really means is that God says He will never let you down and never walk off and leave you. The next verse says, 'The Lord is my helper; I will not be afraid . . .' Do you believe God will take care of you, Tammy?"

She wiped her tears and meekly, but honestly, said, "Yes, but right now I'd rather have Brad." We both laughed, but I saw a new confidence in her eyes. Tammy needed an older woman to remind her to hold on to her faith and to let go of her doubts.

THE MOST IMPORTANT QUESTION JESUS ASKED

As Jesus and the disciples were heading out for the villages around Caesarea Philippi, He asked them, "Who do the people say I am?" (Mark 8:27).

The disciples responded that some people thought He was John the Baptist and others thought He was Elijah, and still others thought He was one of the prophets. Jesus then asked them, "And you — what are you saying about me? Who am I?" (verse 29).

Peter gave the answer. "You are the Christ, the Messiah" (verse 29).

Probably the most important question Jesus ever asked was, "Who am I?" If the disciples got the right answer to *that* question, they understood His purpose for coming and they would understand their mission when He was gone. As we invest time in people, we need to be sure they understand *who Jesus is*. If they believe He was a great teacher, an extraordinary humanitarian, and a compassionate person, they have not yet come to know Him personally. Once they can acknowledge, as Peter did, "He is Christ, the Messiah — *my* Messiah," they are on their way to a personal relationship with God.

A few years ago *USA Today* published a unique weekend insert with a cover story titled "Who Was Jesus?" The article quoted many religion scholars who were responding to questions like, Was Jesus married? Was He a scholar? Was He a carpenter? What was His message? What does His message mean to people in the modern world? After all of these questions were addressed, a conservative clergyman is quoted as saying, "It's really a matter of whether you believe in God or not."[7]

I had been working with a young mom in my Bible study class who had come to know the Lord just two years earlier. She was struggling with questions like, "Was Jonah *really* swallowed by a great fish?" And "Do I have to believe the *whole* Bible is true and without error in its original writings if I believe *most* of it is true?" She had honest questions. I got out this article and asked her who she thought Jesus was. The ensuing discussion became the catalyst for her to feel comfortable to talk openly about her doubts and concerns regarding whether or not the Bible represented absolute truth.

ASKING GOOD QUESTIONS

Knowing how to ask the right question is an important part of being a woman of influence. Here are some guidelines for asking questions that can be life-changing.

KNOW YOUR AUDIENCE

Jesus seemed to "read" His audience and then form a question that was perfect for that person. He had a *confrontational* question for the Pharisee: "Did John's baptism come from heaven or men?"; a *tender* question for the woman taken in adultery: "Where are your accusers?"; and a *revealing* question for the disciples: "Who do you say that I am?"

As we begin mentoring younger women, we need to know our "audience." And getting to know a woman God has put in your life is one of the great joys of the journey.

Here are some questions I use when I'm getting to know a woman I am mentoring:

- What were your growing-up years like?
- What is your best memory of your father? Your mother?
- What is your favorite old movie?
- What kind of music do you like?
- How did your family celebrate Christmas?
- In what part of your life do you feel vulnerable?
- What one thing would you like to do before you die?
- What keeps you from being as close to the Lord as you'd like to be?

The most important question you can ask people is, *How did you come to know Christ?* Their enthusiasm — or lack of it — will tell you whether or not the person is passionate about her walk with the Lord.

ASK QUESTIONS THAT CAN'T BE ANSWERED WITH

A "YES" OR A "NO"

The best coaches and teachers learn how to ask questions that require more than a quick, trite answer. Journalist Leola Floren says,

> *My friend and lifelong mentor, Arline Floren Proctor, specializes in asking the right questions. When I'm struggling to deal with a tough situation, she points me in the right direction by asking, "What does the Scripture say about this?" And when the issue is of a more personal or emotional nature, the question is likely to be, "How may I pray for you?" Those two key questions . . . immediately shift the focus back to where it belongs: on our Father in Heaven.*[8]

Arline's questions also can't be answered with a simple "yes" or "no." All of us have been in conversations with people who give short answers or very quick "yes" or "no" answers. We feel like the burden of the entire conversation is on us—and normally it doesn't last too long. Good questions ask for a descriptive response, an emotional reaction, or a statement of opinion on issues, values, or dreams.

Here are some questions I ask that can't be answered with a "yes" or "no":

- What are your strengths? Your weaknesses?
- If you had a completely free day, what would you do?
- What are your hobbies, interests, and passions?
- If money were not an issue, what would you do with the rest of your life?
- What's the biggest roadblock between you and your dream?

- What would you change about yourself if you had the chance?
- If you could interview any historical person, who would it be and what would you ask?
- In what two specific areas would you like to see yourself grow during the next one to three years?
- What is the biggest answer to prayer you've ever experienced?
- What is your favorite Scripture verse and why does it mean so much to you?
- What do you like best about your job? Least?
- How can I help you?
- What would you like to do for God in your lifetime?
- How can I pray for you?

Our opportunities for influencing people will grow and our personal impact on individuals will multiply as we ask questions that are provocative, timely, important, and inspired by the example of Christ.

Ask Questions at Teachable Moments

Let's take another look at the question Jesus asked of Peter when he tried to walk on water and was sinking: *Why did you doubt?* This question reminded Peter of who Jesus was. It got him to lift his eyes off the waves and wind and onto the God who had the power to silence the wind and waves. What a powerful moment this was in Peter's life — and the lesson was one he was not likely to forget anytime soon.

A situation does not have to be life-threatening to be a teachable moment; teachable moments occur at any time when a person is particularly vulnerable and open. Typically, the younger the person, the more impressionable she is. Throughout most of this book, we've been talking about making an impact on adults or teenagers, but I want to point out that mothers of young children are women of influence as well. In fact, mothers are perhaps the most effective mentors of all — and young children probably have more teachable moments than the typical adult. If you are the mother of small children, I encourage you to pray and be open to ways you can influence your child to be passionate about Jesus.

Recording artist Kim Moore and her daughter, Brittany, were in the car one day when a pop song came on the radio. They both knew the words and instantly began singing. Halfway through the song Kim wondered if Brittany had sifted the lyric of the song through the God-teaching she'd had. As the song finished, Kim said, "Britt, what does that song really say?"

Britt's quick response to the question was an encouragement to Kim. "Well, Mom, it says that it doesn't matter who you are, or what you've done with your life, or what kind of friends you have, as long as you love me. And I think that's the most ridiculous thing I've ever heard. Sometimes I wonder what people are thinking when they write these songs. Someday, when I start dating, I want to know *everything* about the guys that I go out with. It *really* matters who they are and what they've done."

Kim was smiling from her side of the car. Brittany was definitely *sifting*. That day Kim used a teachable moment to ask a question that reinforced important biblical teaching.

A Question for You

Without a doubt, Jesus was a master at asking questions. Even as He hung on the cross, He asked a gut-wrenching question, "My God, my God, why have you forsaken me? Why are you so far from saving me, so far from the words of my groaning?" (Psalm 22:1, NIV).

At that moment God the Father was separated from God the Son so that He could become the sin-bearer of the world. *Why* did God forsake His Son while He died on the cross? The answer to the question is obvious. Because He loves you and me. Plain and simple.

A chapter about the principle of asking questions should definitely end with a question. As you come to grips with the love Christ has for you, will you consider becoming a person who influences the lives of others *intentionally*? Who will *you* tell that Jesus Christ has transformed your life?

Chapter Seven

THE PRINCIPLE OF COMPASSION

Compassion is a sign of a truly great and generous heart. Compassion is understanding the troubles of others, coupled with an urgent desire to help. Man naturally is not compassionate. It is an attribute he must learn by living and by his own experiences. It is cultivating an ability to put [ourselves] in the other [person's] shoes, remembering that all facts and circumstances influencing the other [person] cannot be known to [us].[1]

—MEGIDDO MESSAGE

I MET RUTH WINSLOW ON the other side of the world. She was attending a retreat at which I was speaking for the Evangelical Community Church of Hong Kong. A missionary, Ruth works as a health care professional and vocational counselor, primarily with people who have been cured of leprosy. Even though these precious people no longer have the disease, they are still marked and considered "detestable" because the drug that cures leprosy also leaves a huge scar on their faces and limbs. Many in Asia are still forced to live as outcasts in government-designated areas of mainland China.

Ruth's heart broke as she visited these outcasts in their makeshift houses with dirt floors. Even though they have received physical healing, many are not able to get jobs or make a decent wage. Most have few possessions and suffer greatly from the emotional pain of being shunned by society. But God spoke to Ruth and called her to help these dear people in a very practical and tangible way — she determined to equip them with the skill and means to earn an income.

After hours and hours of paperwork and red tape, Ruth arranged for sewing machines to be brought into one of these villages. Once the machines arrived, Ruth taught the adults how to make quilts for babies. With the help of numerous mission organizations, many of these quilts are being marketed and sold in the United States.

Ruth's face lit up as she told me of the hope and sense of purpose that this task has nurtured in these people. She went on to tell me the following story. One day she was cleaning the ulcerated feet of one of the men in the village. He'd had leprosy for years, and his feet were extremely disfigured. To have his feet touched, let alone cleaned by someone who had never had the disease, must have been an unusual experience. Looking up, his eyes met hers and he whispered, "Thank you."

Ruth's instant response was, "Thank Jesus."

He paused, looked her in the eyes again, and said, "*You* are Jesus."

Jesus told His disciples, "What a huge harvest! . . . How few workers! On your knees and pray for harvest hands!" (Matthew 9:37). Ruth is one of those "harvest hands." Through her ministry in leper colonies, she demonstrates the meaning of compassion. Not only was her heart saddened by the plight of these people, she did something about it. Like Jesus, she was not afraid to touch people who have long been considered untouchable.

If we want to influence lives as Jesus did, we, too, must have a compassionate heart.

LEARNING FROM THE MASTER

Compassion is the heart's response to a person's need combined with a helping hand that offers mercy and grace. The word *compassion* means "to have pity (and) a feeling of distress from the ills of others, to suffer with another . . . to alleviate the consequences of sin or suffering in the lives of others . . . to moderate one's anger (and) treat with mildness, moderation, and gentleness."[2]

Ruth Harms Calkin describes compassion in the following poem:

He sat there in the corridor
Of the convalescent hospital
Trying desperately
To maneuver his wheelchair.

His bony fingers trembled.
A tattered slipper fell off his foot.
I asked if I might help him.
He nodded, and then began to weep.

For a brief moment I put my arms
Around his sagging shoulders.
Then I wheeled him down the narrow hall
To his small warm room.

He thanked me as best he could.
Then he added nervously
"I hope somebody someday will help you
Like you just helped me."

Lord, I hope so, too.[3]

But before a person can communicate compassion, he or she must see another's woundedness and be saddened by it.

JESUS NOTICED PEOPLE'S NEEDS

Over and over, the Gospels tell how Jesus' heart broke with compassion for people.

*Then Jesus made a circuit of all the towns and villages. He
taught in their meeting places, reported kingdom news,
and healed their diseased bodies, healed their bruised
and hurt lives. When he looked out over the crowds,
his heart broke. So confused and aimless they were, like
sheep with no shepherd. (Matthew 9:35-37)*

The text says, "When he *looked out* over the crowds." The passage
doesn't tell us how Jesus felt, but we can imagine that He had been
walking for miles and miles. He must have been exhausted after days of
teaching and healing people, but instead of getting irritated or feeling
hassled, Jesus *noticed* the people's confusion and neediness. He *noticed*
people who needed healing, both spiritually and physically.

When the Pharisees criticized Him for spending so much time with
the outcasts of the day — tax collectors and sinners — Jesus replied, "It
is not the healthy who need a doctor, but the sick" (Matthew 9:12, NIV).
Jesus sought out people who needed compassion. They were the very
people He came to heal and save.

Just a few chapters later we find another example of how Jesus was
deeply moved by people's suffering. He had just been told that John the
Baptist had been beheaded.

*When Jesus got the news, he slipped away by boat to an
out-of-the-way place by himself. But unsuccessfully—someone saw him and the word got around. Soon a lot of people
from the nearby villages walked around the lake to where
he was. When he saw them coming, he was overcome with
pity and healed their sick. (Matthew 14:13-14)*

I have often read this passage, but only recently did I read it in context. John the Baptist was Jesus' cousin and His forerunner. How difficult it must have been for Jesus to hear that this man whom He loved had been so brutally murdered. But someone saw Jesus and quickly spread the word, "Jesus is here! Jesus is here!" Had I been in Jesus' position, I probably would have rowed the boat until I was far from shore so I could mourn alone, but that's not what Jesus did. He landed the boat, saw the crowd, and the Bible says, "He had compassion on them and healed their sick" (Matthew 14:14, NIV).

How different that is from most of us! On the way home from a retreat a few months ago, I lugged my carry-ons to my assigned seat on the aircraft, shoved my garment bag into the overhead compartment, and fell into my aisle seat. As I was putting my briefcase underneath the seat in front of me, I caught a side glance of the woman next to me. She had graying hair, and she was nervously clutching her purse. I figured she hadn't flown much. By the look on her face, I knew opening a conversation could mean a nonstop chat.

Exhausted after speaking at a three-day conference, I had looked forward to a nap on the plane before my ninety-minute drive home from the airport. I smiled and nodded in her direction, and then buckled my seat belt and closed my eyes, indicating I intended to sleep.

My plan worked. I had my nap and avoided a conversation. Much later, the pilot's voice came over the loudspeaker, announcing our descent. Opening my eyes, I glanced in the woman's direction. As soon as we made eye contact, she said, "I just buried my sister yesterday."

"Oh, I'm so sorry to hear about your loss," I said.

She continued, "We buried our mother a year ago this week. There's not much to live for anymore."

At that moment the wheels of the plane hit the runway, and I knew our flight was almost over. My words of hope were delivered too late and too rushed. The two of us gathered up our belongings and parted, still strangers.

I don't know if this woman knew Jesus or not because I didn't take the time to speak with her earlier in the trip. She had wanted to talk. I had wanted to sleep. And because I failed to see people as Jesus saw people, I lost an opportunity to touch this woman's heart with Jesus' love and compassion.

Touch Can Communicate Compassion

Throughout the Gospels, the concepts of *compassion* and *touch* frequently appear together in passages that show Jesus ministering to people. For instance, Matthew 9 tells the story of two blind men who approached Jesus and cried, "Mercy, Son of David! Mercy on us!" (verse 27). Jesus first asked them if they really believed He could heal them. When they responded positively, "*He touched their eyes* and said, 'Become what you believe.' It happened. They saw" (verses 29-30, emphasis added).

In Mark 8, after Jesus and the disciples arrived at Bethsaida, we read:

> Some people brought a sightless man and begged Jesus to give him a healing touch. Taking him by the hand, he led him out of the village. He put spit in the man's eyes, laid hands on him, and asked, "Do you see anything?"
>
> He looked up. "I see men. They look like walking trees." So Jesus laid hands on his eyes again. The man looked hard and realized that he had recovered perfect

sight, saw everything in bright, twenty-twenty focus.
(verses 22-25, emphasis added)

Can you see these compassionate friends begging Jesus — pleading with Him — to touch their friend? Jesus does, and their friend is healed.

Jesus, by example, taught that having a compassionate heart often includes a healing touch. One of the most powerful illustrations of how healing a touch can be is found in Matthew 8.

> *Jesus came down the mountain with the cheers of the crowd still ringing in his ears. Then a leper appeared and went to his knees before Jesus, praying, "Master, if you want to, you can heal my body."*
>
> *Jesus reached out and touched him, saying, "I want to. Be clean." Then and there, all signs of the leprosy were gone. Jesus said, "Don't talk about this all over town. Just quietly present your healed body to the priest, along with the appropriate expressions of thanks to God. Your cleansed and grateful life, not your words, will bear witness to what I have done." (verses 1-4)*

Have you ever wondered what it would *feel* like to be a leper? What it would be like to say goodbye to your spouse, children, and friends and to be banished from their world forever? To be shunned, ridiculed, and excluded? To experience loneliness and isolation? To be an outcast? In his book *Just Like Jesus,* Max Lucado powerfully portrays what the leper in Matthew 8 might have thought and felt the day Jesus touched him and healed him. The following is written from the leper's viewpoint.

> *For five years no one touched me. No one. Not one person. Not my wife. Not my child. Not my friends. No one touched me. They saw me. They spoke to me. I sensed love in their voices. I saw concern in their eyes. But I didn't feel their touch. There was no touch. . . .*
>
> *What is common to you, I coveted. Handshakes. Warm embraces. A tap on the shoulder to get my attention. A kiss on the lips to steal a heart. Such moments were taken from my world. No one touched me. No one bumped into me. What I would have given to be bumped into, to be caught in a crowd, for my shoulder to brush against another's. But for five years it has not happened. How could it? I was not allowed on the streets. Even the rabbis kept their distance from me. I was not permitted in my synagogue. Not even welcome in my own house.*
>
> *I was untouchable. I was a leper. And no one touched me. Until today.*[4]

Lucado goes on to explain why leprosy was so dreaded in Jesus' day.

> *The condition rendered the body a mass of ulcers and decay. Fingers would curl and gnarl. Blotches of skin would discolor and stink. Certain types of leprosy would numb nerve endings, leading to a loss of fingers, toes, even a whole foot or hand. Leprosy was death by inches.*

> *The social consequences were as severe as the physical. Considered contagious, the leper was quarantined, banished to a leper colony.*
>
> *In Scripture the leper is symbolic of the ultimate outcast: infected by a condition he did not seek, rejected by those he knew, avoided by people he did not know, condemned to a future he could not bear. And in the memory of each outcast must have been the day he was forced to face the truth: life would never be the same.[5]*

It's important to note that Jesus' touch was not what healed the man. His *word* wiped out the disease. But His touch — prior to the word that brought healing — was pure compassion. Jesus' compassionate touch validated the man's worth, affirmed his personhood, and revived his hope.

You and I may not have the same ability to heal people as Jesus did, but we can offer a "healing touch," whether it be through a warm hug, a simple squeeze of an arm, a gentle touch on a shoulder, or a lingering handshake.

Last weekend I was picked up at the San Diego airport by a breast cancer survivor. I was speaking at a women's retreat not far away, and this woman had volunteered to provide my transportation. As she drove, she told me how alone she sometimes had felt and how difficult it had been to go through the diagnosis, surgery, and subsequent treatment for her cancer. Before I left the retreat, this dear woman handed me a note, stating: "The year of cancer was the most joyful year of my life. . . . one of my friends came over and bathed me after my second surgery. I told her the story of Jesus washing the disciples' feet and we were both in tears." As I read, tears came to my eyes over the loving, compassionate — and healing — touch of this caring and wise friend.

A REFLECTION OF THE FATHER'S HEART

Many of the stories Jesus told are stories that reflect the heart of a compassionate and loving Father, but none better than the story of a father who had two sons. The younger son wanted his inheritance immediately. The father divided the property between the two sons and the undisciplined son left and wasted everything he had. Finally, reduced to slopping pigs, he realized his father's farmhands had a better life than he had.

He came home to tell his father he didn't deserve to be his son and that he wanted to work for him as a hired hand. "But while he was still a long way off, his father saw him and was filled with compassion for him; he ran to his son, threw his arms around him and kissed him" (Luke 15:20, NIV). The son confessed his sin, but the father wasn't listening. He was so excited and happy that his son had returned, he was already making plans for a celebration.

When the older son came in from the fields and learned that his father had ordered a feast in honor of his wayward brother's safe return home, he was so angry he stalked off and refused to join in. His father came out and tried to talk to him, but he wouldn't listen. The son said, "Look how many years I've stayed here serving you, never giving you one moment of grief, but have you ever thrown a party for me and my friends? Then this son of yours who has thrown away your money on whores shows up and you go all out with a feast!"

His father said, "Son, you don't understand. You're with me all the time, and everything that is mine is yours — but this is a wonderful time, and we had to celebrate. This brother of yours was dead, and he's alive! He was lost, and he's found!" (verses 28-31).

When I first heard this story, I empathized with the older son — perhaps because as a teen, I never rebelled or caused my parents grief. I felt it was unfair that the brother who squandered his inheritance received such royal treatment. Why would the father throw such a huge party for a son who had disappointed him so severely?

Today, however, I realize this story defines true compassion. The father of the prodigal son loved both sons equally, but he showed compassion to the one who needed it. We don't show compassion because someone in our life deserves it, earns it, merits it, or works for it. And if our hearts reflect an attitude of harshness, unforgiveness, criticism, judgment, hardness, or enmity — especially to those who have repented — we are not treating people as Jesus did. We may still influence them . . . but not in a way that edifies them or brings God glory!

How Can You and I Show Compassion?

Corrie ten Boom, who has been a mentor to me through her books and example, once asked, "What have you done today that only a Christian would have done?"[6] If you and I would learn to consistently — daily — ask ourselves this question, and would pray that God would make us more like Him, we would become women who influence others with our gift of compassion.

Jess Moody offers further insight about how to show compassion.

Did you ever take a real trip down inside the broken heart of a friend? To feel the sob of the soul—the raw, red

*crucible of emotional agony? To have this become almost
as much yours as that of your soul-crushed neighbor?
Then, to sit down with him—and silently weep? This is
the beginning of compassion.*[7]

If we are going to become women of compassion, we need to do
the following:

- See a woman's need.
- Feel her pain (or need).
- Get involved (instead of walking by or passing the buck).
- Weep with her (show empathy).
- Extend support and help—hands-on, if possible. (Remember, Jesus *touched* people wherever He went.)
- Wait with the woman (in spirit or in person) until her needy situation is resolved.

When I first met Kathe Wunnenberg, I had no idea that God
would use her to help me become more compassionate. She came into
my life like a whirlwind. She had read one of my books and spontane-
ously called my home. By the end of the call, she had invited me to meet
with her in Phoenix on my next Western speaking trip. Within a short
time, our friendship became a long-distance mentoring relationship.

Kathe was a former marketing executive who had left her position
to accept God's call to minister to professional women and to be more
available to care for her adopted son, Jake. To her great surprise, she
became pregnant when Jake was six years old. She was thirty-seven.
She and her husband were ecstatic until the day they received some

distressing news. Kathe was in the doctor's office having an ultrasound when the nurse grew silent and excused herself. The doctor came in, and after checking for himself, solemnly announced, "I'm so sorry. Medical science has no conclusive answers as to why this condition occurs. Your baby is not developing properly. This baby has no chance of survival."

At the very moment the doctor recommended termination of the pregnancy, the baby kicked Kathe's ribs. Her immediate response was, "Doctor, this baby is very much alive. We may not know why these things happen, but we know who controls the outcome." Termination of the pregnancy was out of the question.

Kathe and her husband were told the baby was anencephalic and that he would be born without a skull and brain and would not live long (if at all) after birth. Day after day she had her devotions at the breakfast table, laid her hands on her growing womb, and prayed that God would miraculously form a brain inside her baby's head.

When she told me the news, my heart ached for my friend. As Kathe's e-mails and faxed reports on her progress arrived, I covered her with prayer. And I waited with Kathe for the birth of this baby — her gift from God. The due date was August 8. On the night before, I went to bed very late, but awakened in the middle of the night. I felt compelled to send Kathe a faxed note. This is what I wrote:

> *My Dear Friend,*
>
> *You have been on my mind and in my heart during the past three days. I have had the remarkable experience of praying for you during a portion of every waking hour.*
>
> *Yesterday I was acutely aware of your August 8 due date. I went to bed last night at about 11:30 P.M. and slept*

until 2:30 A.M. When I woke up at this unusual hour, I was so alert and wide awake I got out of bed and went downstairs. I thought perhaps you were in labor and God wanted me to intercede on your behalf — and I prayed for you fervently. I lapsed into intermittent praying and dozing — and then at 6:20 A.M. I heard the familiar ring of my fax machine.

When I read your note and realized what time it was in Phoenix, I knew you had been awake much of the night, too. . . . What an awesome experience it was to receive your precious note during this extraordinary night of praying for you. My eyes are filled with tears to think God "knit our hearts together" — from one end of the country to the other during this night of "waiting and praying" for His miracle.

Kathe's letter to me read:

My labor of love is nearly here, Carol. . . . So many miracles have already occurred. . . . Each day God provides incredible encouragement.

I have planned a praise celebration for after the baby's birth. The date will be 2-3 days after, unless I have physical complications. Jake is very excited about this event and he wants to have balloons there and he wants us to sing "Jesus Loves Me" and "Jesus Loves the Little Children of the World." . . . A praise team will lead worship and our pastor will deliver a short message . . . whether we have a memorial service or a baby dedication, we will praise God. Rich and I have discussed all possible outcomes and actions, knowing that God does not see this as a lack of faith or doubt, but as a necessary part of life. We are still expecting to hold a healthy, whole child.

What a journey this has been, my friend! I have laughed, cried, learned the necessity of silence and solitude, bonded with my unborn baby, released control, and allowed others to encourage me. . . . Thanks for your friendship, encouragement, and prayers. I love you!

Kathe

On August 22, John Samuel was born. Within a few hours, there was a flurry of angel wings as these messengers of God ushered a tiny newcomer directly into the waiting arms of Jesus.

God allowed me to love and encourage Kathe during this time of waiting, disappointment, and grief. I couldn't "fix" her situation. I couldn't change the circumstances. I couldn't even physically be with her. But I could feel her pain, weep with her, and let her know my heart was broken, too. I encouraged her, prayed for her, and waited with her for the outcome.

IDEAS FOR PRACTICING COMPASSION

Compassion is often very practical. Here are some ideas about how you can show more compassion to someone you are mentoring. (Or consider inviting her to join you in giving one of these compassionate gifts to someone else who needs encouragement.)

- If she has young children, offer to babysit so she can have a few peaceful hours alone or go shopping with a friend.
- Cook a meal for her family or household on her busiest day of the week. If possible, deliver the meal, serve it, and stay to clean up the mess.
- Purchase two registrations for a women's conference and surprise someone with an unexpected inspirational weekend away from home. Help her to arrange for child care if she has small children.
- Find out about any days that trigger sadness in the lives of those you are mentoring—the anniversary of the death of a child, parent, or spouse. Send flowers or a card to let the person know you are covering her with prayer on this particular day. If possible, take her to lunch and ask questions that give her an opportunity to talk about a departed loved one.
- Invite her to go with you when you take a mentally or physically challenged person to the store or to an appointment.
- If her funds are limited, place a sack of groceries on her doorstep, ring the doorbell, and leave. Have a note inside the grocery sack that says, "From someone who loves you and hopes you enjoy every bite."
- Invite her to accompany you on a visit to a convalescent home. If she has musical gifts, encourage her to sing to some of the patients. Take turns reading short inspirational or humorous stories to individual patients.
- Ask her, "What's the toughest situation you've had to deal with this week?" Listen carefully as she answers, and give her a safe place to vent frustrations, fears, and concerns. Offer genuine

compassion, biblical counsel, and then take the time to pray
with her about what she's struggling with.

You could probably think of twenty more compassionate acts of
kindness. Remember, compassion is not simply feeling sad about someone's pain or circumstances, it is also *doing something* to alleviate the pain.
One author says, "When you help someone else up the hill, you reach
the top yourself."[8]

If you are ready for an adventure, try doing three intentional acts
of compassion this week — and watch how God works in your heart as
well as in the hearts of those lives you touch!

WHAT WOULD YOU HAVE DONE?

I would like to close this chapter with one final story. On a cold
December day in New York City, a ten-year-old boy stood in front of a
shoe store on Broadway. He was barefoot, peering through the window,
and shivering with cold. A woman approached the boy and said, "My,
little fellow, why are you looking so earnestly in that window?"

"I was asking God to give me a pair of shoes," the boy replied.

The woman took him by the hand, went into the store, and asked
the clerk to get half a dozen pairs of socks for the boy. She then asked if
he could give her a basin of water and a towel. The clerk quickly brought
her the requested items.

She took the little fellow to the back part of the store. Removing
her gloves, she knelt down, washed his little feet and dried them with
a towel. By this time the clerk had returned with the socks. Placing
one pair of the socks on the boy's feet, she then purchased him a pair

of shoes, and tying up the remaining pairs of socks, gave them to him. She patted him on the head and said, "No doubt, young man, you feel more comfortable now?"

As she turned to go, the astonished lad caught her by the hand, and looking up in her face with tears in his eyes, answered the question with these words, "Lady, are you God's wife?"[9]

This woman practiced what Jesus talked about in Matthew 25:38: "I was shivering and you gave me clothes." When we show compassion to the people around us, we are Jesus to them. Jesus said, "I'm telling the solemn truth: Whenever you failed to do one of these things to some- one who was being overlooked or ignored, that was me — you failed to do it to me" (verse 40).

Chapter Eight

THE PRINCIPLE OF UNCONDITIONAL LOVE

There is nothing else that can expand the human soul, actualize the human potential for growth, or bring a person into the full possession of life more than a love which is unconditional.[1]

— JOHN POWELL

I FOUGHT BACK TEARS AS I held the hotel phone to my ear. "Mom and Dad," J.P. was saying, "my naval orders have changed and I have to report to Surface Warfare Officers' School in Newport, Rhode Island, on September 8. April and I are in love and we want to be married right away so we can go to Newport together." He went on, "We were thinking we could get married next weekend right here in Orlando."

My mind and emotions were whirling. *How could this be happening?* Our son was telling us he wanted to marry a woman we had never met — *next* weekend. Gene and I had already made plans to fly to Orlando, Florida, on Labor Day weekend to meet April for the first time — and now J.P. was telling us they wanted to get married immediately! My breathing was labored, and I found myself stifling a sob.

All I could focus on was that April had been previously married and had two children. I had prayed for years that J.P. would marry a virgin and that he would save himself for her and that she would save herself for him. *A divorced woman with two children did not fit what I thought was the answer to my prayers!*

J.P. and April had met through the singles' program in their church. They told us, "Neither of us had any hidden agendas or ulterior motives, but just a desire for friendship. Over the months that friendship developed to the point of becoming *best* friends. We believe God wants us together and we want to live out the rest of our lives together."

Their minds were definitely made up. Within minutes Gene and I knew we could cause a rift that would last a lifetime — or we could give our son and his bride our blessing, encouragement, and support. So with fear in our hearts, we persuaded them to wait three weeks and get married in our hometown so that we could help plan a very speedy wedding.

I hung up the phone and sobbed. I was speaking in Denver for two more days. The last thing I wanted to do was to stand in front of a group of people and tell them how much God loved them and wanted to meet their needs. He didn't seem to be meeting *my* needs. I was confused, hurting, and disappointed.

With a heavy heart, I plunged into wedding plans as soon as I returned home. Within days the invitations were printed and the envelopes were addressed and mailed. I anxiously awaited the day I would meet my soon-to-be daughter-in-law. Those days seemed like weeks, but the moment finally arrived. J.P.'s arm encircled April's waist as she walked with him through the front door of our home, followed by six-year-old Chelsea and three-year-old Hannah.

I liked April immediately. It was obvious that she loved my son deeply and that he loved her. Not long after they arrived, Chelsea came running up to me unexpectedly. She took my hand in her two hands and began kissing it as she looked up with her big, beautiful, brown eyes and said, "You're my new favorite Grammy." Hannah got up every morning and sang songs about how much she loved Jesus in between bites of cereal. These little girls were *precious*. My heart was melting.

As the next few days unfolded, I heard more of April's story. As she unveiled the unhappy and hurtful details of her background and her fears for her children, I realized she was a woman of great personal strength, faith in God, and love for her family. Instead of allowing the pain of the past to make her resentful, angry, and embittered, she chose to trust God in the middle of impossible circumstances. She knew how hard this speedy marriage would be for the parents of an only child, and she was trying her best to make it easier for us.

The day before the wedding, I told April I had prayed for J.P.'s future spouse since he was very young. I told her, "That means I've been praying for you for many years." Both of us had tears in our eyes as we talked about God's protection through prayer. She thoughtfully said, "During the worst of all I went through, I always knew God had something better for me." I had known April for only two weeks, but I understood why my son cared for her so deeply. She is passionately committed to Christ and has raised her two adorable little girls to love Jesus.

I realized that for years I had placed "conditions" on who I would allow to get this close to me — to us! Could it be that God was teaching me a new definition of unconditional love and grace through April, Chelsea, and Hannah?[2]

LEARNING FROM THE MASTER

No one has ever loved us more completely or undeservedly than Jesus. When He lived on this earth, He didn't love some people and not others. He didn't love people because of how they treated Him or because of what they thought of Him. He loved everyone equally and unequivocally. Some people were surprised by His love and others never even recognized His love. Certainly, none of us *deserve* His love. Just ask the Samaritan woman.

One day Jesus left the Judean countryside, and on His way back to

Galilee, He passed through Samaria. He came into Sychar, a Samaritan village that bordered the field Jacob had given to his son, Joseph. Jacob's well was still there. Jesus was exhausted and sat down by the well.

A Samaritan woman came to draw water and Jesus said to her, "Would you give me a drink of water?" (John 4:7). She was taken aback. Why was a Jew asking a Samaritan woman for a drink?

Jesus told her that if she knew the generosity of God and who He was, she would be asking *Him* for a drink, and He would give her fresh, living water. She could see He had no bucket, and she didn't understand how He would be able to get this *living* water. Jesus then said, "Everyone who drinks this water will get thirsty again and again. Anyone who drinks the water I give will never thirst — not ever. The water I give will be an artesian spring within — gushing fountains of endless life" (verse 13).

The woman asked Jesus for this water that would take away her thirst *forever*. He told her to call her husband and then to come back. She responded that she had no husband, and Jesus replied that her words were true — she had five husbands and the man she was living with wasn't her spouse.

On this, *The Quest Study Bible* comments: "Divorce in the Jewish-Samaritan culture could only be initiated by the husband, who had to state publicly that his wife was unclean, unlovable, or incapable of fulfilling her wifely duties. Divorce therefore shamed a woman. And now she was most likely living with her current partner simply to avoid starvation."[3]

THE NEGATIVE IMPACT OF "CONDITIONAL LOVE"

What had happened to this woman's sense of significance when society announced that she was an unclean, undesirable woman who was not capable of fulfilling her duties as a wife — *five times?* I meet many women who have endured similar rejection, and their wounds are deep. Can you feel the pain beneath the following words?

- "My husband ran away with his secretary two days before our twentieth anniversary."
- "I'm single and never feel like my parents love me as much as my siblings who married and produced grandchildren for them. They treat me as if I'm incomplete without a husband, and I'm sick of hearing them ask, 'Are there any new men in your life?'"
- "I was in an automobile accident during my first year of marriage and have deep scars on my face. One day in the middle of an argument my husband yelled, 'You old scar-faced woman— you can't do anything right.' Now, whenever he looks at me, I know he sees a scar-faced woman and our relationship has been permanently damaged."
- "My mother-in-law has never accepted me and loved me as her daughter because I didn't come from the right social background to be worthy of her son. She will never know the joy she's missed by rejecting me."
- "I was a promiscuous woman for many years before I met Jesus, and people in my church can't seem to forget the woman I used to be and accept me as the forgiven woman I am today."
- "My husband always pinches the skin under my upper arm and says, 'You're not going to get fat on me, are you? It's hard to make love to an overweight woman.' For years I've lived with the fear of losing his love if my beauty fades or if I gain weight as my metabolism changes."

Each of these women was hurt by someone whose love was conditional. Most of us, at some time or another, have endured rejection, unforgiveness, mistreatment, or inappropriate, unloving responses from people we longed to have love us. Most of us have experienced the feeling of being unlovable in at least one area of our lives. Our unspoken cry is *Please love me!* When you and I listen to people's stories without judging them, we are taking the first step in practicing unconditional love.

Jesus talked to the woman at the well about the racial and religious prejudices that separated the Jews and the Samaritans. How healing His words must have been!

> "The time is coming—it has, in fact, come—when what you're called will not matter and where you go to worship will not matter.
>
> It's who you are and the way you live that count before God. Your worship must engage your spirit in the pursuit of truth. That's the kind of people the Father is out looking for: those who are simply and honestly themselves before him in their worship." (John 4:23)

Before their conversation ended, Jesus revealed that He was the Messiah. But when the disciples came back, they were shocked that Jesus was talking with *that kind* of a woman. "No one said what they were all thinking, but their faces showed it" (verse 27). The woman took the hint and left in such a hurry she forgot her water pot. But when she got to the village, she told the people, "'Come see a man who knew all about the things I did, who knows me inside and out. Do you think this could be the Messiah?' And they went out to see for themselves" (verse 29).

Jesus loved this woman unconditionally — and because He did, she had a new confidence. Her immediate response was to tell people about the man she met who knew her "inside and out." She planted seeds of faith in the hearts of all she spoke to.

WHAT DOES UNCONDITIONAL LOVE LOOK LIKE?

One of the most powerful statements on how to love was written by Paul. He was a man who understood hatred, anger, vengeance, and bitterness. He had persecuted and destroyed believers before he was transformed by the power of God's unconditional love. Paul's words offer further insight on how we can love like Jesus loves.

Love never gives up.
Love cares more for others than for self.
Love doesn't want what it doesn't have.
Love doesn't strut,
Doesn't have a swelled head,
Doesn't force itself on others,
Isn't always "me first,"
Doesn't fly off the handle,
Doesn't keep score of the sins of others,
Doesn't revel when others grovel,
Takes pleasure in the flowering of truth,
Puts up with anything,
Trusts God always,
Always looks for the best,

Never looks back,
But keeps going to the end. (1 Corinthians 13:4-7)

Augustine said, "What does love look like? It has the hands to help others. It has the feet to hasten to the poor and needy. It has eyes to see misery and want. It has the ears to hear the sighs and sorrows of men. That is what love looks like."[4] We cannot practice the principle of unconditional love apart from practicing the principle of compassion. Compassion and unconditional love go hand in hand.

Of unconditional love, John Powell writes:

> *To choose love as a life principle means that my basic mind-set or question must be: What is the loving thing to be, to do, to say? My consistent response to each of life's events, to each person who enters and touches my life, to each demand on my time and nerves and heart, must somehow be transformed into an act of love. However, in the last analysis, it is this "Yes!" that opens me to God. Choosing love as a life principle widens the chalice of my soul, so that God can pour into me His gifts and graces and powers. . . .[5]*

THE THREE STAGES OF LOVING OTHERS

Powell continues,

> *In the process of loving there are three important stages or moments:*

1. *Kindness: a warm assurance that "I am on your side. I care about you."*

2. *Encouragement: a strong reassurance of your own strength . . .*

3. *Challenge: a loving but firm exhortation to action. . . . the first thing love must do is communicate these three things: I truly care about you. I really want your happiness and I will do all I can to assure it. You are a uniquely valuable person.*⁶

Jesus' treatment of the Samaritan woman illustrates this definition. It was *kind* for Jesus — a Jew — to engage a Samaritan woman in conversation. Jews had only disdain for Samaritans, whom they saw as inferior and unworthy. Jesus' behavior told her she was a valuable person. He *encouraged* her by affirming her truthfulness about the fact that she had no husband. And by the end of their conversation, He had *challenged* her to discover that He was indeed the true Messiah.

Unconditional love is not concerned about what someone *did;* it does not use *appearance* as a measuring stick for personal worth. Nor does unconditional love throw the past into the face of someone who hasn't asked for our forgiveness, even if that person wronged us. In fact, Jesus said, "I'm telling you to love your enemies. Let them bring out the best in you, not the worst. . . . If all you do is love the lovable, do you expect a bonus? Anybody can do that. . . . In a word, what I'm saying is, *Grow up.* You're kingdom subjects. Now live like it" (Matthew 5:44,46,48).

Jesus Demonstrated His Teachings on Love

Jesus also said, "This is my command: Love one another the way I loved you. This is the very best way to love. Put your life on the line for your friends" (John 15:12-13). Giving your life out of love for someone else is the highest demonstration of unconditional love.

> *This is how much God loved the world: He gave his Son, his one and only Son. And this is why: so that no one need be destroyed; by believing in him, anyone can have a whole and lasting life. God didn't go to all the trouble of sending his Son merely to point an accusing finger, telling the world how bad it was. He came to help, to put the world right again. Anyone who trusts in him is acquitted; anyone who refuses to trust him has long since been under the death sentence without knowing it. And why? Because of that person's failure to believe in the one-of-a-kind Son of God when introduced to him. (John 3:16-18)*

Picture this: Jesus was God, yet He humbled Himself to become one cell in a woman's womb. He grew to maturity, went into public ministry, and men that He created yelled, "You're not the Messiah! You are not the man you claim to be!" The religious leaders of the day accused Him of blasphemy and schemed to get rid of Him. Eventually, one of His own disciples betrayed Him. He was beaten, mocked, and spat upon. Finally, He faced a death so horrible it was usually reserved for foreigners and slaves — death by crucifixion. God's Son was nailed to a cross by His hands and feet to die a criminal's death. Because a man would die quickly of suffocation if hung only by his hands, the knees were flexed and nails were put through the feet, allowing him to live for hours and sometimes days. During crucifixion the body would involuntarily push up on the nails in the feet to get the breath to sustain life, sending excruciating pain through the nerve endings, thus prolonging the suffering.

The sinless Son of God could have said, "No, I will not demean myself and go through this pain." But He didn't. God proved His love on the Cross. When Christ hung, and bled, and died, it was God saying to the world, "I love you."[7] That's unconditional love. We never deserved it. We couldn't do enough to earn it. We simply receive it.

If you're reading this book and for the first time you realize how much God loves you — personally — and you desire to begin a walk of faith with Him, pause for just a moment. Bow your head and pray, "Lord, I acknowledge that I need You in my life. I'm tired of trying to pick myself up by my own ability. I need Your forgiveness, and I realize when Jesus died on the cross it was because He loved me *unconditionally* and paid the price for my wrongdoing. I know He did not stay dead — He rose from the grave. I confess my sin and invite Jesus to be my Savior. Come into my life and help me to live for You. In Jesus' name. Amen."

If you just prayed that prayer, you have received the unconditional love and forgiveness of God and you are part of a new family — God's family.

LOVING OTHERS LIKE JESUS DID

How, then, can you and I practice this principle and ignite it in others?

I was captured by the scenario in Luke 15 that pointed out who Jesus hung out with: "By this time a lot of men and women of doubtful reputation were hanging around Jesus, listening intently. The Pharisees and religion scholars were not pleased, not at all pleased. They growled, 'He takes in sinners and eats meals with them, treating them like old friends'" (verses 1-2).

I believe that it is a mark of spiritual maturity when Christians have a few people of "doubtful reputation" within our circle of friends. The words "doubtful reputation" may sound a bit severe, but I think we need to ask women we mentor to occasionally spend time with us when we are with nonChristians who may have a drastically different lifestyle than they are used to.

During my early years of teaching, I developed a friendship with another teacher who had been "dumped" by her husband so he could go back to partying like a single guy. Whenever I accompanied Lori in her car or visited in her home, she always played Carly Simon's song, "You're So Vain." She made a point of saying she played this song over and over again because it reminded her of the selfish, uncaring, egocentric, self-indulgent clod of a man she had once been married to. Lori needed the Lord if she was ever going to become free from the anger, rejection, and hopelessness of her situation.

One afternoon I invited Sarah, a young woman I was mentoring, to come over for coffee in order to meet Lori. Sarah was from a conservative Christian home and had recently married.

As soon as Lori arrived, she lit up her first cigarette, even before I had a chance to introduce her to Sarah. The three of us sat at the kitchen table while Lori plunged into the latest story about what she had heard Dan was doing with other women *this* week. While she lit cigarette after cigarette, Sarah would watch the white roll of tobacco go from her lips to the coffee cup saucer she used as an ashtray, and back to her lips.

Sarah appeared shocked when Lori told us she drank a whole six-pack of beer by herself the night before.

I calmly said, "What triggered that response, Lori?"

She responded, "I'm tired of being alone and I'm tired of playing the role of a convenient weekend toy."

"What do you mean?" I inquired.

She told us that for the past ten years, she'd had an annual weekend getaway with a man she had dated while she was in college. She said it all started when he called one day and asked her to meet him at an out-of-state location where he was on a business trip. Even though she was married, she made an excuse to her husband and took a flight to meet her former boyfriend.

Hugging her, the old boyfriend said he had missed her, and that he was "happily" married and had three children—but that didn't mean they couldn't have a lot of fun together. Lori said the two of them had a great time that weekend—gourmet meals, dancing, drinking until the wee hours of the morning, and an affair that made her wish she'd thought twice before marrying someone else. "We *always* have a good time. We *always* sleep together. We *always* say we wish we had married each other. But he *never* says he'll leave his wife and marry me. I feel like I'm a useless plaything. I'm hurt and I'm mad. Aren't I good enough for *anybody* to love?"

When I told Lori that I'd been praying for her every day, she said, "You *have*? *Why* would you do that? My life isn't *worth* being prayed for."

I had shared part of my testimony with her and Lori knew I was "a religious person," as she put it. But this afternoon I was able to tell her the story of the woman at the well and Jesus' response to this woman who felt forsaken and left alone by a series of men. I explained the love Christ had for her and the difference He had made in my life. Lori didn't accept the Lord that day, but as she left, Sarah and I knew God had used this encounter to get her to think about the truth of God's unconditional love.

After Lori's departure, Sarah looked at me and said, "I watched you today while you invited Lori into your home. You let her smoke in your kitchen. You listened to her tell about a ten-year affair. She cussed a lot and she's not someone I would enjoy spending much time with, but I saw you make her feel valued . . . to feel cared for. I know she listened when we talked about God because she first knew that you accepted and loved her as a person. I really don't have any nonChristian friends, but I saw today that if I don't build relationships with people who need to know God's love, I probably won't get to be the one who introduces them to Christ."

That afternoon provided me with a unique opportunity to show unconditional love to Lori, but it also allowed me to positively influence Sarah's life with new ideas on how to reach the people around her for Christ.

CONTEMPORARY APPLICATIONS OF JESUS' TEACHINGS

Here are some other ways of mentoring through the principle of unconditional love:

- When someone with whom you are in a mentoring relationship becomes upset with you or criticizes you, stop for a moment and realize that person probably misunderstood your method, your material, or your motive. Ask God to reveal anything wrong on your part that needs an apology. Take action, if necessary. If there's nothing to apologize for, forgive her anyway—first in your heart, and then by doing a conscious act of kindness for her. The closer mentoring relationships become, the more potential there is for doing something that can produce a misunderstanding that needs love and forgiveness.

- Do you know a woman who has made poor or wrong choices that have caused her to be rejected and criticized by others? Go over the story of the woman at the well and affirm that it is "who you are" and "the way you live now" that matters to God. Affirm His love and your love for her. Treat her with kindness and compassion. Don't be one of her judges. Tell her of the relentless love of Jesus and His willingness to forgive again and again.

- Introduce women you are seeking to influence to the idea of doing "random acts of kindness" to demonstrate the love of Christ to the people around you. I recently had a woman with me when I purchased a "VeggieTales" video for another woman who does child care in her home. I knew this woman had recently lost her mother to cancer and that she felt discouraged. We stopped by her home to say hello and told her we brought a little surprise that we hoped would let her know we loved her and that would give her something inspirational for the children. You would have thought we brought her a dozen roses. Her face lit up and she hugged both of us as she said, "It's good to know somebody loves me and understands what I've been going through lately."

The young friend who was with me was surprised at how much this small kindness meant to the woman. After we got back in the car, she turned in my direction and said, "Wow! It makes me want to think up one thing a day that will touch the lives of people with Jesus' love. It's so much fun!" She was definitely learning that it's not just the recipient of loving acts who reaps the benefit.

LETTING GOD LOVE YOU

Some of you might be struggling with the idea of loving others unconditionally because you feel that you have never been loved that way yourself. You know the amazing story of the ultimate price Jesus paid to demonstrate His unconditional love and to save us from eternal destruction, but practicing the *giving* and *receiving* of His love on a daily basis is sometimes challenging.

In his outstanding book *The Jesus I Never Knew*, Philip Yancey writes:

> *I remember a long night sitting in uncomfortable Naugahyde chairs in O'Hare Airport, waiting impatiently for a flight that was delayed for five hours. I happened to be next to a wise woman who was traveling to the same conference. The long delay and the late hour combined to create a melancholy mood, and in five hours we had time to share all the dysfunctions of childhood, our disappointments with the church, our questions of faith. I was writing the book* Disappointment with God *at the time, and I felt burdened by other people's pains and sorrows,*

doubts and unanswered prayers.

My companion listened to me in silence for a very long time, and then out of nowhere she asked a question that has always stayed with me. "Philip, do you ever just let God love you?" She said, "It's pretty important, I think."

I realized with a start that she had brought to light a gaping hole in my spiritual life. For all my absorption in the Christian faith, I had missed the most important message of all. The story of Jesus is the story of a celebration, a story of love. It involves pain and disappointment, yes, for God as well as for us. But Jesus embodies the promise of a God who will go to any length to win us back. Not the least of Jesus' accomplishments is that He made us somehow lovable to God.[8]

That honest account of a "chance" five-hour meeting in an airport made me think. If we are lovable to God — so lovable that He sacrificed His own Son for us — that means we are women of significance, dignity, honor, and great worth. That sense of security should give us the confidence to begin giving unconditional love to others.

THE GIFT THAT KEEPS ON GIVING

In two weeks my son, his new wife, and my two granddaughters will be here for Christmas. I look forward to the privilege of being a mentor to April. What I would have missed if I had chosen not to love and accept her as my son's bride! With every phone call I love her more and realize that Jesus is the Lord of new beginnings. Unconditional love is the gift that keeps on giving. When we receive it because Jesus first gave it to us, our natural response is to give it to others. And it keeps on giving . . . and giving . . . and giving.

Chapter Nine

THE PRINCIPLE OF CASTING VISION

Vision is essential for survival. It is spawned by faith, sustained by hope, sparked by imagination, and strengthened by enthusiasm. It is greater than sight, deeper than a dream, broader than an idea. Vision encompasses vast vistas outside the realm of the predictable, the safe, the expected. No wonder we perish without it![1]

— CHARLES R. SWINDOLL

R AY WAS THE FIRST ADULT outside of my family who told me I had potential to do something great for God. He was the state director of Youth for Christ. My parents had moved to Sandusky, Michigan, and I was in my first year of university studies out of state. I was not looking forward to spending the summer in an unfamiliar place.

Within a week of my return home, Ray asked if I would join a Teen Team for the summer with five other university students, and I accepted. We performed upbeat, contemporary music that attracted crowds on a beach, at a county fair, or in a city park. We approached people after our free concerts with a little booklet called "The Balanced Life Quiz." Our purpose was to introduce people to Christ after leading them through the key questions in the quiz.

I enjoyed this new opportunity at first, but soon there was a major wrinkle in my comfort zone. All of the other team members had been in international touring music groups and their musical talents were enviable. We had two trombonists, a trumpeter, a flutist, and a keyboard artist, and all of them could solo on the vocals, as well as with their instruments. The audience would shout out the name of a popular song and these people could play it flawlessly — in any key, without music — and do stylistic variations within the piece, from jazz to country, or classical to calypso.

I was out of my league musically and felt miserable. In spite of my desire to invest my summer in something of lasting value, I knew I didn't fit. Ray sensed my uneasiness and pulled me aside. I told him I loved being on the team, but I didn't want to hurt the group's musical reputation. Ray looked me directly in the eyes, and said, "Carol, the reason we brought this team together is that there are so many teenagers in this area who need Christ. You have an ability to relate to them. The team we've put together has incredible musical talent, but you have *personality!*"

He went on: "Carol, our main purpose is to introduce teenagers to personal faith in Christ, and your contribution to the team is outstanding. You concisely introduce the songs and tell humorous stories that keep people laughing and listening. And when you mingle in the crowd afterward, it's awesome to see how people relate to you. They actually cluster around while you are telling them how to establish a meaningful relationship with Christ. You have a remarkable gift of evangelism."

When Ray finished, my self-esteem was intact. He made me believe I had something worthwhile to contribute to the team's ministry and that I was not only *needed*, but *wanted*. When he established that my main function on the team was *personality*, the rest of the team applauded my gifts. All of us understood our individual purposes. We redesigned the concerts to let the multi-talented instrumentalists and vocalists be featured in the programs, and I participated only in the group numbers. As soon as we finished our concerts, I hit the crowd and built relationships with people who needed to know Jesus. It was a winning combination!

I recently wrote down how Ray's visionary leadership had influenced me:

He made me feel valuable. By affirming my strength (personality) and my spiritual gift (evangelism), he helped me realize I made an essential contribution to the team.

He painted a clear picture of our mission and my contribution. I finally understood that our goal was not to do professional concerts. Our goal was evangelism, and my place on the team was key if we were going to fulfill our purpose.

He set me up for success, not failure. He freed me from having to do something I wasn't good at, and encouraged me to do what I could do best — meet people and tell them about Jesus.

He inspired me. I felt privileged to communicate truth to people who needed a fresh touch from God in their lives. I knew there was nothing more important to do with my time and energy. This was *kingdom work!*

He gave enough training to make us feel prepared, but enough freedom to help us accomplish the mission in creative, contemporary ways. Community Bible Study Teaching Director Margaret Frost says, "People are encouraged to become their best when you hold a crown just a little above their heads and ask them to grow into it."[2] That's what Ray did. Our team had the freedom to evaluate each new audience and make changes if we believed a variation in our regular program would reach a particular group more effectively. When we made a mistake or failed, he was there to help us try again. He coached us and affirmed us through the process.

Most individuals do not think they are *special* enough to make a difference. We need to affirm our belief in their ability to change the world with their unique gifts. When we do, we are following Jesus' example.

LEARNING FROM THE MASTER

Jesus lived outside the box of how other people thought He should live, and He instead focused on His purpose. He came from a place of blazing glory to live and die among people He created who didn't recognize who He was. His zeal for God's honor propelled Him on His downward journey to incarnation — God becoming human flesh. Jesus ignited the hearts of His disciples with God's vision for redeeming this world.

Pastor Bill Hybels speculates that Jesus must have thought, "I can continue to do everything, or I can build the leadership abilities of people who can take the baton when I return to the Father."[3] Hybels continues, "When you have an exciting, God-inspired vision and you invite others to help bring that vision to life, most will be grateful that you asked for their help. . . . Jesus concerned Himself with far more than preaching and healing — He invested heavily in developing the people who were following Him."[4]

How did Jesus ignite a vision within the hearts of His disciples?

JESUS SAW PEOPLE'S POTENTIAL

During the time Jesus lived, the rabbis of the day never went out and recruited students. They sat back and students came to them; the higher your status as a rabbi, the more students would come to listen to your teaching. However, Jesus broke the rules. He *recruited* people; He had an amazing ability to look at them and see their God-given potential. He took unlikely candidates — fishermen and tax collectors — who were not about to attach themselves to rabbinic schools and turned them into His dedicated disciples.

When I pray about who God wants me to mentor intentionally, I ask that I would be able to look past the woman's current ministry position and past her education (or lack of it) and see her potential. Perhaps she doesn't look like it today, but she may be the next Henrietta Mears or Corrie ten Boom or Elisabeth Elliot. We need to ask God to give us lenses through which we can see the potential of the people around us, to quicken our mind and touch our spirit with discernment as we seek to invest time and training in helping someone else carry the message of Christ.

JESUS GAVE THEM A VISION OF WHAT THEY COULD DO

After Peter recognized that Jesus was the Christ, the Messiah, the Son of the living God, Jesus said to him,

> *"My Father in heaven, God himself, let you in on this secret of who I really am. And now I'm going to tell you who you are, really are. You are Peter, a rock. This is the rock on which I will put together my church, a church so expansive with energy that not even the gates of hell will be able to keep it out. And that's not all. You will have complete and free access to God's kingdom, keys to open any and every door: no more barriers between heaven and earth, earth and heaven." (Matthew 16:17-19)*

Talk about building confidence in a person and casting a vision!

When we work with people and name the potential we see in them, it helps them to envision their personal worth to God and to us, even if we say it with a different twist:

- "Susan, you have great administrative ability."

- "Kathy, you have a unique ability to negotiate peace in the middle of dissenting opinions on the women's ministries team."
- "Jan, when you led in prayer at our last committee meeting, God used you to create an atmosphere of unity and spiritual oneness."
- "Heather, you have a remarkable ability to make the Bible study lectures come alive. You are an outstanding researcher and you have a gift for teaching."

We have to be careful about jumping to conclusions when we affirm people regarding their God-given potential, but our prayerful verbalization of the gifts we see in others helps build their confidence and give them a vision of what their future ministry might be. Just ask Sherrie.

Sherrie Eldridge, founder of Jewel Among Jewels Adoption Network, Inc., writes, "Seven years ago, a good friend encouraged me to submit an eighty-page account of my recent reunion with my birth-mother to Traci Mullins, then senior acquisitions editor of NavPress."

Though Sherrie was terrified at the thought, she submitted her piece. About six weeks later, Traci wrote a letter to Sherrie saying, "Your account was so intriguing, I couldn't put it down. I read it cover to cover!" Sherrie was encouraged. But then came the follow-up comments. "You need some time to heal before you share your story with others. May God gently guide you along His healing path."

Five years passed, and during that time Sherrie grieved her loss, screamed her anger, and cried her tears. God opened doors for her to tell her story in magazines; she founded a national organization for adoptees and wrote support group materials.

When the time seemed right, she again contacted Traci, now president of Eclipse Editorial Services, and hired her as her agent-editor. Within a few weeks, a publishing house offered Sherrie a contract. Sherrie said,

> *I found Traci to be a tough coach and a tender shepherd for this first-time author. She continually cast a vision for me during the writing process by exhorting me to be the very best I could be. She would say: "Aim high. Amplify your thoughts. Remember your readers and the tremendous impact this book is going to have on their lives." When we got to the place that Traci called the labor pains of birthing a book, she was there as the midwife, holding my hand, reassuring me that all authors must go through this and that the pain would pass.*

Sherrie wasn't so sure. Finally, as the thoughts came together and the book was completed, Traci said she felt like a proud mama duck. When the book was finished, she sent Sherrie this letter:

> *My Dear Baby Duck,*
>
> *I think back so many years ago to a tiny duck named Sherrie who approached me with an idea for a book about her painful experience of reuniting with her birthmother. I knew she needed to write, write, write . . . for her own sake. For a catharsis. For her healing. She needed a little more time in the "nest" where she could be safe before heading out into the big wide world where everyone*

would know her story. She needed to mine for the jewels
deep within her own soul before she could begin handing
them out as gifts to others.

And now . . . she has transformed from a tiny duck
into a lovely swan, beautiful and confident and strong
enough to help other tiny ducks learn to fly. She has meta-
morphosed from a fledgling writer with journal and pen
to a brilliant, real author who's even mastering the com-
puter! Most of all, she has become a whole woman God is
using in profound ways . . . which have only begun . . .

Love,
Mama Duck

Sherrie says she will forever be grateful to Traci for casting a vision for her when she was too broken and bruised to do it for herself. Traci's vision helped Sherrie make her lifetime dream of writing a book come true.

All of us have opportunities to cast a vision for others, and God will allow us to use our own unique personality and expertise to complete His kingdom work. For Traci, it's encouraging aspiring writers. For me, it's coaching younger speakers. For you, it might be launching a support group for mothers of preschool children or starting a Bible study in your neighborhood because you have accepted Jesus' challenge to "Go out and train everyone you meet. . . . Then instruct them in the practice of all I have commanded you. I'll be with you as you do this, day after day after day, right up to the end of the age" (Matthew 28:19-20).

I love that Jesus reminded His disciples He would be with them. When we take on the visionary task of challenging others to live out their purpose, we are not alone. He is with us "day after day after day."

JESUS PREPARED HIS FOLLOWERS FOR WHAT TO EXPECT

Jesus developed the people who were following Him. In Matthew 10, He gave them some very specific instructions and how they should respond:

Start where you are with what you see. "It's best to start small. Give a cool cup of water to someone who is thirsty, for instance" (verse 42).

"Do not go among the Gentiles . . ." It wasn't that He didn't care about the Gentiles, but because no foundational work had been done with them, He knew He would be setting His disciples up for failure if they went there with no experience (verse 5, NIV).

There will be times when people are unresponsive and your ministry has no fruit. Don't get "all beaten up" over that; expect it and move on. "When you knock on a door, be courteous in your greeting. If they welcome you, be gentle in your conversation. If they don't welcome you, quietly withdraw. Don't make a scene. Shrug your shoulders and be on your way" (verses 12-14).

Don't be wishy-washy. If you mean business with Me, be committed. "If you don't go all the way with me, through thick and thin, you don't deserve me" (verse 38).

Don't be concerned about yourself. If you look to Me, you'll find Me and your true identity. "If your first concern is to look after yourself, you'll never find yourself. But if you forget about yourself and look to me, you'll find both yourself and me" (verse 39).

You are not alone in this great work. "We are intimately linked in this harvest work. Anyone who accepts what you do, accepts me, the One who sent you. Anyone who accepts what I do accepts my Father, who sent me" (verses 40-41).

Find your niche in My plan. No function is greater than another. "The smallest act of giving or receiving makes you a true apprentice. You won't lose out on a thing" (verse 42).

I want the early experience of ministering to others to be as reward-ing as it can possibly be, so others catch the thrill of being used by God. I warn them there will be people who may not respond positively to their personality or style of ministry, but assure them God will use other people to reach them.

JESUS GAVE THEM A CHALLENGING, VISIONARY TASK

After His resurrection, Jesus appeared to the Eleven as they were eating supper and He said, "Go into the world. Go everywhere and announce the Message of God's good news to one and all" (Mark 16:15). That was a massive, extraordinary challenge! Yet we know the disciples succeeded. The vision of Christ is still being carried on today — two thousand years later.

If we follow the example of Christ and inspire twelve people to mentally visualize the mission Jesus called us to do, we will mobilize a future generation of people who will live out their purpose on this earth. Bobb Biehl, author of *Mentoring*, sets forth this challenge:

> *Pause for sixty seconds and try to imagine the implica-tions of this:*
>
> *You mentor 12, who mentor 12, equals 144!*
> *who mentor 12, equals 1,728!*
> *who mentor 12, equals 20,736!*
> *who mentor 12, equals 248,832!*
> *who mentor 12, equals 2,985,984!*

Is an unbroken chain of mentors realistic? Probably not!
But the point is clear. Even if only a small fraction of
protégés follow through by mentoring someone else, a sig-
nificant difference will be made in the number of leaders
in the next few centuries — or until the Lord returns.[5]

As women of influence, how can we give others the challenging, visionary task of announcing God's good news to one and all? I've found the best way is to be involved in doing it myself.

Several years ago, I led a home Bible study with the theme of helping women get prepared to share their faith. Several weeks into the study, I challenged the women to intentionally verbalize their faith to someone God put in their path the following week. I told them I would take on the same challenge and we would report back at the next Bible study about what happened.

Days later I left for a four-day insurance convention with my husband. One morning Gene had a business meeting and I had a free morning. I walked back into my hotel room after enjoying an early walk on the beach, and the maid was there. She had finished cleaning the bathroom and was about to put clean sheets on the bed. I greeted her warmly and said, "I'd like to help you make the bed."

She glanced up with an incredulous look on her face and said, "Why, thank you, Ma'am. I've worked at this hotel for five years and no one has ever done that before."

As we pulled the bedspread over the pillows, I asked her about her family. She was a single mom raising two small children on a limited income. Life was hard, and she was struggling to make ends meet. As she finished up in the room, I had the perfect opportunity to tell her about my faith in Jesus Christ. She hung on every word. And at the end of our time together, she prayed to receive Christ. I took her address, hugged her goodbye, and promised to be in touch with her by mail.

At our next Bible study, all the group could talk about were the exciting encounters they had with people the previous week. Sally talked to her hairdresser about an answer to prayer. Bonnie asked her neighbor over for coffee and shared her testimony at the kitchen table. Jean had a unique opportunity to voice her faith with her son's third-grade teacher. One after the other, they told of the ways God opened doors for them to "announce the message of God's good news."

I told them what happened when I presented the gospel to the maid in South Carolina, and they wanted to drop everything and pray for this young woman and her children. This one-week "experiment" provided a momentum that continued to grow throughout the rest of the Bible study and beyond. They caught the vision.

VISIONARY PEOPLE OF INFLUENCE

Over the past two years I've asked women to tell me about the people who helped them to "catch and hold onto" the vision of what God was designing them to become. If you want to be inspired, listen to the stories that follow.

Julie Baker is a recording artist and the founder and president of the Christian arena events called "Time Out for Women." She tells of the influence of her high school speech teacher, Miss Harvey.

Miss Harvey spent four years modeling for me the teacher
I would one day become. She coached me through variety

shows, plays, and musicals, helping me to keep in mind that the most important thing about "presenting" is to sincerely care for each person in my audience. If I care more for them than for myself, I can channel my nervousness into enthusiasm and rapport. It's not unusual for me to see Miss Harvey seated in my audiences today, halfway back on the center aisle, beaming her smile of encouragement. Today I opened a letter from her: "Oh, Julie, I am so proud of you! Oh how special you are — how talented. . . . I just love you dearly and you have surely proved that 'They can conquer who believe they can,' and 'Enthusiasm is the x-ray of the soul. . . .'" Her influence and encouragement accompany each of my endeavors. And sometimes I hear the faint echo of her voice, "Julie, I'm so proud of you."

Miss Harvey reminds all of us that women who cast vision are lifetime encouragers.

Jayne Clark is director of women's ministries in her church in Topeka, Kansas. She says several of her mentors are the widows who sit on the back row of the auditorium for the 8:00 A.M. Sunday service.

They're the women who taught Sunday school classes, worked in the nursery, led vacation Bible school, sang in the choir, and spent endless hours preparing care packages for our missionaries for many years. They helped me catch the vision for leadership and service.

A few weeks ago I was greeting these ladies when

something caught my eye. One of them had a tarnished rhinestone brooch pinned crookedly on her faded flower dress. It was in the shape of a heart and on the inside was spelled "Jesus." I commented about how unusual and lovely it was. This adorable lady looked up to my face and with one hand holding mine and the other grasping the brooch, she whispered, "I love Him! I love Him! I love Him!"

These women remind us that the most effective mentors help us to catch the vision of serving wherever God opens a door. It might not be on a huge platform or in a visible position — but we serve because we love Jesus. For most of us, service starts with a neighborhood Bible study, or working in the church nursery, or teaching in a Sunday school classroom. And in the process of saying "yes" to the opportunities we have today, we catch the vision of the importance of faithfulness in the small tasks.

Bernadine Johnson is a gifted pianist and the composer and arranger of numerous piano performance books. She says the person who cast the vision of what she could become was her sixth-grade teacher, Mr. Farinella.

Mr. Farinella was my first male teacher, and he just sparkled when he smiled. One day he heard me play "Moon River" on the piano. He liked that song so much that every once in a while he would wheel the piano into our classroom and ask me to play it for him. I remember feeling pretty special, and for the first time in my life I realized that somebody liked hearing me play the piano and thought I was good at it—somebody other than a relative!

Mr. Farinella reinforces the fact that mentors who cast vision affirm the giftedness of those they influence.

Martha Strickland is the former director of training and education for CB International, a Christian mission organization. She met her mentor, Dr. Paula Martinez, when she was a student at Wheaton College. Martha describes a professor who gave her a vision of her purpose:

She was the first professor who took a personal interest in me. She spent hours coaching and affirming me in my quest as a new teacher. During the spring semester she chose me to be her first teacher's assistant. Even in that position, I was not just given the "grunge" duties, like photocopying and simple clerical work. She entrusted me to work on her post-doctoral research.

After I graduated, she kept in contact and supported me as I went overseas as a teacher. I came back on my first furlough exhausted, broken, and doubting my future as a teacher. I called Dr. Martinez and after hearing my shaky voice, she cleared her schedule and picked me up for lunch the next day. She gave me the gift of a listening ear as I poured out my struggles. Then she surprised me by taking me to the classroom of a master teacher in the area. She deposited me at the door, talked to the teacher, and left.

I sat in that classroom and watched this master teacher at work for hours. I saw her use the same methods I had

used in the mission school; I realized her challenges in the
classroom matched some of those I had faced. I entered
that classroom weary, broken, and full of self-doubt, but I
left with renewed hope. I am so grateful for a mentor who
helped me to recover my lost vision and gave me the cour-
age to keep pioneering in new areas of education.

Dr. Paula Martinez demonstrates the importance of casting vision during the inevitable times when those we mentor experience failure. Good mentors restore hope, courage, and the ability to see a better future.

WHAT HAPPENS WHEN YOU ACT ON GOD'S VISION FOR YOUR LIFE?

In 1983 I was finishing another year as a Bible Study Fellowship leader. I loved teaching God's Word; I enjoyed the relationships with the women on the staff team. Women who had been church attendees were becoming Christ followers. But God's Spirit was stirring within me. I was sensing a "creative restlessness."

The next week I looked over the large audience of women from a variety of backgrounds and realized how many of them had a powerful story to tell, but they didn't know how to put their testimony together. Others had a deep love for Scripture, but didn't know how to teach. As I prayed about the restlessness I was feeling, God reminded me that my university degrees were in speech education and in communication arts. After years of teaching speech and God's Word, perhaps I could equip people with communication skills that would further the kingdom of God.

Within six months I developed training materials and launched the communications training seminar that is now called "Speak Up with Confidence." It started with fifteen women in my living room who were learning how to share their personal spiritual journeys in spoken form for the first time, and now the seminar is presented to thousands of men and women in cities across the United States and Canada.

It was Henrietta Mears who said, "There is no magic in small plans. When I consider my ministry, I think of the world. Anything less than that would not be worthy of Christ nor of His will for my life. . . . What you *are* is God's gift to you. What you can *become* is your gift to Him."[6]

What happens when you catch a vision of what God might be doing in your life and then you act on that dream?

You experience *risk*. In my case I was giving up the most meaningful Christian ministry I'd ever been involved in — teaching Bible Study Fellowship classes. I couldn't do that and begin training a much smaller group of women who wanted to learn how to communicate effectively. When I left my job as the teaching leader, I felt like I was risking the possibility of giving up my sense of spiritual fulfillment.

You experience *fear.* The Enemy approached me with hundreds of reasons why I could never be qualified to teach this group of women how to speak. *Who did I think I was?* For a while I wondered if launching this communications seminar was just an ego trip that would wind up making me feel like an idiot.

You experience *total dependence on God.* When you start feeling weak, you start seeking His face through prayer and Bible study. The more I prayed, the more I felt an urgency to use my gifts to train others how to speak. The more I read the Bible, the more God confirmed through Scripture that I was following His visionary will for my life in launching this seminar.

You experience *joy*. There can be no greater joy than living out your purpose. As I moved forward in the direction in which God had been pointing my vision, I sensed the joy of "living in the smile of God's approval." I call it the *eureka* of knowing you are in God's will.

I could almost see Him cheering me on and waving banners from the heavens, yelling, "I'm putting a demanding and challenging task in front of you. There will be times when you think you can't do it, but that's okay. I'll be here to coach you and problem-solve with you. I'll be your inspiration because your work is My work — kingdom work — and we're in this together. I'll celebrate with you every time one of the people you are training stands up in front of an audience and speaks for Me."

You receive *more assignments*. The Christian life is never static. It's always changing, always moving, always animated, always compelling. As God confirms your vision, new doors open. Current tasks are delegated to people who are ready to risk saying "yes" to Him. And "creative restlessness" returns. But this time, you know it's the Holy Spirit saying, "Listen up! I have another demanding but fulfilling task for you to do."

Last year God led me to begin a new arm of Speak Up Ministries, and Speak Up Speaker Services was launched. Our office now places over 150 gifted Christian communicators with retreats, conferences, and keynote speaking opportunities where their services are needed. I would never have believed that God would allow me to mentor Christian speakers who are looking for direction in their ministries. But He did. And Jesus' challenge in Mark 16:15 to "Go into the world. Go everywhere and announce the Message of God's good news to one and all" is being actualized by many young Christian speakers who are willing to say, "Lord, I'm available. Reveal Your vision to me. I am no longer content to live a safe Christian life. Move me out of my comfort zone. I long for an adventure in trusting You. I hang my weakness on Your strength. I want to live out the principles Jesus modeled. I want to be a woman of influence who is making a lasting impact on others."

WILL YOU JOIN THE ADVENTURE?

If we want to impact lives as Jesus did, we will give people opportunities to grow, and then encourage and help them if they fail. It means taking the time to pray with them, train them, and encourage them. Sometimes it means watching them fail the first time they try a new task. Author and speaker Jan Johnson writes, "When pondering dreams, many conclude: *I could never do this. . . . I'm not clever enough . . . it'll never succeed. . . .* But failure is normal, even essential. It is the fertile ground from which success arises. . . . The question is not whether you've made some mistakes or failed in the past, but whether you'll let fear keep you from trying."[7]

Let's not let fear hold us back. Let's be more like Jesus. Let's see people like He saw them — people with great potential. Remember, making a lasting impact on others doesn't have to do with *you*, it has to do with how much you become like *Jesus*.

If you and I want to become women of influence, we will do what Jesus did.

1. Spend time alone with God.
2. Walk and talk with people so that we can influence them through impact moments.

3. Tell stories and use word pictures to make spiritual truth come alive.

4. Ask people questions, especially ones that don't have "yes" or "no" answers.

5. Show compassion.

6. Practice unconditional love.

7. Cast the vision of what Jesus can do through the life of someone who is willing to give her potential to Him.

I know my life is a journey, and at times I think I've arrived at the place of influence God wants me to be in for the rest of my life. Then I look at the landscape and see the faces of people I've met along the way — people who need compassion, unconditional love, a method for spending time alone with God, a key question to help them find answers, a personal story of Jesus' ability to change a life, or perhaps just an impact moment because they have never met a Christian before. And I realize, "I am here . . . but I'm not where I'm going," because the more I look at the example of Christ, the more I get a vision of the new challenges He has for me.

Author and speaker Os Guinness might have said it best:

> Do you have a reason for being, a focused sense of purpose in your life? Or is your life the product of shifting resolutions and the myriad pull of forces outside yourself? Do you want to go beyond success to significance? Have you come to realize that self-reliance always falls short and that world-denying solutions provide no answer in the end? Listen to Jesus of Nazareth; answer His call.[8]

Becoming a woman of influence is costly, risky, and time-consuming, but there can be no greater joy than knowing you have obediently begun to impact others by shaping hearts to the image of Jesus Christ. Come join the greatest adventure of your life!

NINE-WEEK BIBLE STUDY FOR BECOMING A WOMAN OF INFLUENCE

Dear Friend,

I'm filled with excitement about what God is going to do in your life as you participate in this study. My life has been profoundly altered as I have studied the life of Christ and observed how He influenced the people closest to Him. Elisabeth Elliott once said, "We are created to glorify Him as long as we live on this planet, and to enjoy Him for the rest of eternity. Our task is simply to trust and obey. This is what it means to love and worship Him. Jesus came to show us how that can be done."[1]

No one can come to an understanding of *what* He did, and *why* He came, without being changed herself. I tend to mimic the behavior and speech patterns of people I admire, and the more I see Jesus, the more I want to be like Him — to share in His purpose — impacting the lives of others *intentionally*. Seeing people like He saw them. Seeing people as they really are — with the pain of rejection, the fear of the future, the questions pertaining to faith and life, and the honest expressions of doubt. Real people. Vulnerable people. But people with great potential.

If we desire to be women who make a difference in the lives of others, we need to consistently gain godly wisdom by studying biblical principles and then purposefully take the time to memorize scripture.

Linda Dillow says, "Bible study is good, but *memorizing* and *meditating* on God's Word are the best ways to place His Word in your heart and mind."[2]

If you are studying this material on your own, it will be helpful. However, if you decide to study with one additional person or with a small group of women, it will be even more beneficial. When we build accountability and the dynamic of discussion into our understanding of the principles Jesus taught, it ignites follow-through commitment to practice what we are learning. It also adds fun, excitement, and spiritual energy to the learning process. The unexpected benefit is the development of lifelong friendships with other women.

Imagine what it would have been like to slip on a pair of sandals and follow the Son of God around for three years. Watching Him respond to a touch in the crowd from a woman who longed for healing. Protecting Him from the masses of people who wanted to see another miracle. Hurting inside as the Pharisees mocked Him and tried to twist His words and meanings. Smiling as He stopped to hold a child in His lap. Hearing His gentle words to the woman at the well. Eavesdropping as He prayed. Observing as He responded to tough questions. Gasping as He touched *another* leper. Aware of His power. Awed by His teaching. Inspired by His stories. Forever changed by His mission.

If you are ready for a life-changing adventure, pray before you begin this study.

> *Lord, I long to live for something that will last forever. I acknowledge Your power, majesty, and unconditional love for me. I am humbled to think You would use such an ordinary woman to affect the lives of others. Help*

me to apply the principles You taught and modeled for making a lasting difference in the lives of others. Keep me focused on biblical truth, personal integrity, and gut-level honesty as I enter into this study. Bring younger women into my life that you want me to influence. Lord, I'm available to You. Use me. Break me. Mold me. Place Your indelible imprint on my life. In Jesus' name. Amen.

I'm praying that you will be transformed as you participate in this study of the principles Jesus modeled as He mentored His disciples. We can make a lasting impact on others as we follow the example of Jesus Christ.

Carol Kent

WEEK ONE

Read chapter 1, "Impacting Lives As Jesus Did."

1. Read Psalm 1, which is a description of the person who delights in the Law of the Lord and meditates on truth.

   a. Based on this Scripture, make a list of the benefits of delighting in the Law of the Lord.

   b. What does this passage say will happen to the wicked?

2. Memorize Psalm 1:1-3. Write the verses on a 3 x 5 card and rehearse them in the car, at your kitchen sink, during a brisk walk, or between phone calls. Pray the verses back to God. (Sometimes it helps to write out your prayers.) For example:

   > *Lord, help me to avoid following the bad counsel of people who give ungodly advice and help me to stay clear of people who pull me down with their inappropriate actions and negative speech patterns. Help me to delight in Your Word and to give serious thought to Your teaching. Help my character to be as strong as a tree planted by a stream, yielding spiritual fruit and maintaining healthy leaves. I know this pattern will allow me to prosper in my walk with You and will be a positive example to the people I influence.*

3. J. Oswald Sanders said, "Spirituality is not easy to define, but its presence or absence can easily be discerned.... It is the power to change the atmosphere by one's presence, the unconscious influence that makes Christ and spiritual things real to others."[3] In your own words, write out a contemporary definition of

what you think "spirituality" is.

4. As a young adult, I was profoundly influenced by the example of Corrie ten Boom. I was particularly gripped by the way she modeled forgiveness and unconditional love. Use your Bible concordance to look up three verses each on forgiveness and love. Choose one of the verses in each category that challenges you and write it out.

   a. Forgiveness

   b. Love

   c. Which of these virtues do you need to put to work in your life as you respond to someone you are close to?

5. Read the story of Meghan and her teacher, Mr. Ottley, on pages 16-17. Carefully look at the inscription this influential teacher wrote in her high school yearbook.

   a. What do you think gave Meghan so much hope through Mr. Ottley's words and pointed her to Christ?

   b. What older person (outside of your family) impacted your life in a positive, spiritually challenging way? Describe what this individual did to influence the direction of your life. Do you think his or her influence on you was "intentional" or "unintentional"?

6. In John 10:10, Jesus stated the purpose of his life: "I came so they can have real and eternal life, more and better life than they ever dreamed of."

   a. List some of the ways Jesus gave people a better life when He walked on this earth.

   b. Write out a description of how Jesus has impacted your life.

7. The word *influence* has to do with a person's wisdom or force of character that makes a lasting impact on the behavior or choices of

another individual. Jesus powerfully influenced the disciples.

a. Read Matthew 5:1-12 and list eight ways in which Jesus said His followers would be blessed.

b. As you made your list, which method for being blessed is something you have experienced? Describe what happened.

8. Review the following longings. Circle the ones with which you currently identify:

- "I wish I had someone who would mentor me."

- "I long for accountability in a friendship with someone who has known the Lord longer than I have, but the people I know are so busy I don't know who to ask."

- "I wish I knew someone with whom I could share my dreams and who would listen and give me honest feedback."

- "I long to connect with a younger Christian woman who I could encourage, support, and challenge to be her best for Christ."

- "My marriage is less than I had hoped. I thought I was marrying the strong, silent type, but now I know I just married a man who doesn't know how to communicate. Who can I talk to without embarrassing my husband?"

- "My boss has been unfair. I'm not given the respect I should have for my position at work. I need this job, but I need to know how to confront my boss in an appropriate way. Who can I talk to?"

- "I'm a new Christian. I want to learn about the Bible and I long to know how to pray, but I need guidance. Do you know anybody who could work with me on my spiritual growth?"

- "I wish I had a younger woman in my life who would be interested in personal and spiritual growth. I long to help someone else through the hurdles I faced in earlier years."

Take a few minutes to pray about these longings and ask God to meet your needs. If none of the longings applies to this stage of your life, pray for someone you know who is struggling with one of these issues or challenges.

9. Read Psalm 37:4-5. Paraphrase these verses in your own words.

WEEK TWO

Read chapter 2, "Learning from the Master."

1. Read 1 Corinthians 11:1. What do you think Paul meant when he said, "Follow my example, as I follow the example of Christ" (NIV)?

2. Memorize Philippians 3:10. Write the verse on a 3 x 5 card and carry it with you until you master the verse.

   a. Write out what it means to you "to know Christ and the power of his resurrection" (NIV).

   b. What do you think "the fellowship of sharing in his sufferings" (NIV) means?

3. Matthew 10:1 says, "He called his twelve disciples to him and gave them authority to drive out evil spirits and to heal every disease and sickness" (NIV). The needs were great when Jesus walked the earth, and the needs are great today. List some of the challenges you see in the lives of women you know.

4. Read Matthew 14:13. Jesus demonstrated that the key to spiritual power is time alone with God.

   a. Based on this verse, describe Jesus' "quiet time."

   b. What are your current prayer concerns?

5. Jesus often taught important principles in a non-classroom environment during His "walking and talking" moments along a roadside or at an informal gathering of friends. List five incidents you remember from the life of Christ when He made spiritual applications in the middle of an unscheduled encounter.

6. Jesus knew how to capture the attention of His listeners. Read Matthew 13:10-13. What do you learn in these verses about why Jesus

used stories as teaching tools?

7. Jesus knew the power of a well-placed question. Read Luke 18:41.

   a. Why do you think Jesus often asked questions that couldn't be answered with a "yes" or "no"?

   b. Write out a question you have right now that you would appreciate having answered by someone who is spiritually mature and further along in life experience than you are.

8. Look up the word "compassion" in an English language dictionary and in a Bible dictionary.

   a. Write out both meanings.

   b. Read the story of Gene Taylor and the Salvation Army officer on pages 34-35. Why do you think this simple act of compassion was so powerful?

   c. Describe what you think it means to "be Jesus" to someone in today's culture.

9. Read Jeremiah 31:3 and John 8:4-11.

   a. Describe in your own words what the woman caught in the act of adultery must have felt after Jesus demonstrated unconditional love and forgiveness toward her.

   b. Reread Zephaniah 3:17. Describe a time in your life when you sensed that God "delighted" in you.

   c. Write out your prayer of response to God or use the following example as you voice your thoughts to Him.

   Lord, I am honored and sometimes surprised that You delight in me. You have given me a feeling of significance and immeasurable worth. You make me feel like a valued woman. Thank You for quieting my heart with Your love.

To think that You rejoice over me with singing is a precious reminder of Your remarkable joy in calling me Your child. I love You, too. Amen.

10. Jesus lived for only thirty-three years and influenced the lives of a handful of men who so powerfully impacted their culture that the world has never been the same. And He used such ordinary men. It was almost as if He said, "Becoming a person of influence who makes a lasting impact on others doesn't have to do with you, it has to do with how much you become like Me." And then throughout His lifetime He modeled the seven principles we would need to learn to do it the right way.

   a. Read Matthew 28:19-20.

   b. Jesus knew how to cast vision for His followers. In these verses, what are the specific things Jesus told His disciples to do? What assurance did He give them?

11. Reread these seven life-changing principles based on the life of Christ that give us an example of "perfect mentoring":

   • Spending time alone with God, so we have a deepening love relationship with our Father and something of substance to give to others.

   • Making a difference during the impact moments we have with other people through "walking and talking" the way He did.

   • Being quick to tell our own story of how Jesus has transformed our lives, and relating additional meaningful stories that make spiritual truth relevant to people who don't know much about the Bible.

   • Asking people questions that don't have "yes" or "no" answers —

questions that move people to think and to evaluate their spiritual condition.

- Showing compassion by active participation in the lives of others as our hearts are broken by things that break the heart of Christ.

- Practicing unconditional love by choosing to forgive people who don't deserve to be forgiven and letting go of "my right" to exclude someone from my life.

- Casting the vision of what Jesus can do in the life of a person who is willing to give her potential to Him.

  a. Which principle is the most meaningful to you?

  b. Which principle do you currently need to have modeled to you by a mentor?

  c. Which principle have you modeled in the life of a younger woman recently?

  d. As you think about the life of Christ, what impresses you most about the way He influenced His disciples?

WEEK THREE

Read chapter 3, "The Principle of Time Alone with God."

1. Memorize Psalm 119:10-11.
2. Each day this week read Psalm 119:9-16 and pray these Scriptures back to God.
   a. Make a list of the specific actions to which these verses refer that involve your personal time alone with God.
   b. For which of those actions is it most difficult for you to make time?
3. Read Mark 1:21-35. These verses describe twenty-four hours in the life of Christ.
   a. Make a list of every activity Jesus was involved in that day.
   b. What was His priority early the next morning?
4. Read Matthew 9:36-10:1.
   a. Describe Jesus' emotions as He looked over the crowds.
   b. What did Jesus ask His followers to pray for?
   c. Some of the disciples became the answer to their own prayer. Describe a time in your life when you were burdened to pray for a specific need, and God asked *you* to be the one who responded to the prayer request.
5. Read Luke 5:16.
   a. Where did Jesus usually have His "quiet time"?
   b. Describe your favorite place to spend time alone with God.
6. Read Richard Foster's definition of a solitude of the heart on page 46. He said, "There is a solitude of the heart that can be maintained at all times."

a. How does Foster describe this unique spiritual discipline?

b. Do you agree or disagree with the idea that there is a "solitude of the heart" that is possible to be maintained at all times? If you agree, explain how this is possible during the busy activities of each day.

7. Read Matthew 6:5-18. List Jesus' instructions on how we should pray.

8. Describe a time in your life when you failed at doing devotions? What do you think was wrong?

9. Read Luke 11:10-11. Now read the testimony of Jim Cymbala on pages 53-54.

a. How does this story demonstrate the importance of making our prayers personal and direct?

b. Describe the most specific answer to a prayer request you have ever had.

10. Review the four ways discussed on pages 56-58 that we can influence others to spend time with God.

a. List them below and put a check mark next to each you have used to influence someone else.

b. Make an appointment to interview a woman you know who has a lifetime habit of spending time alone with God. Write down questions ahead of time that will help you to make the most of your time with this person.

11. Marlae Gritter encourages women to plan ahead for "DAWG days" (Day Alone With God). Describe what you would do if you had a whole day to concentrate on your spiritual development and personal time with God. Make a list of the activities you would most want to do on your day alone with Him, and then check your calendar. When

could you schedule this opportunity? If you have young children, could you arrange to trade child care responsibilities with a friend? (Even if it can't be a whole day to begin with, try for a morning or an afternoon.)

12. Read Psalm 34. With conversational prayer, take a few minutes to express your love to Him verbally. Delight in His presence. End by singing a song of praise and worship to Him—out loud!

WEEK FOUR

Read chapter 4, "The Principle of Walking and Talking."

1. Read Proverbs 2:1-12. Make a list of the benefits experienced by the person who walks and talks wisely.

2. Memorize Proverbs 2:1-5. Be sure to print these verses on a card that can be carried with you. Review the passage each day this week and rephrase the words from these verses back to God in prayer. You can use your own words or the following example:

> *Lord, I accept Your words and I am diligently trying to memorize Your commands so that my ear will recognize wisdom and my heart will understand truth. I long for insight and understanding, and I'm willing to search the Scriptures to find it. I know my earnest investigation of Your Word will end in understanding and knowing You more intimately. Amen.*

3. Jesus often took advantage of impact moments to teach and influence others as He encountered individuals during the activities of an average day.

   a. After reading chapter 4, describe an impact moment in the life of Christ.

   b. Describe an impact moment you have had with someone else. (This might be with an older, more mature Christian whom God used in your life, or it might be an opportunity you have had to influence someone else at an unexpected moment.)

4. Read Luke 8:40-55. Describe how Jesus turned an interruption into a significant appointment.

5. Read the familiar story about Jesus' visit with Mary and Martha in Luke 10:38-41. In the past week, have you been more like Mary or Martha? Explain.

6. Jesus took His disciples with Him when He traveled and preached. They learned much by watching the way He interacted with people as He healed, told stories, taught object lessons, and gave instruction.

   a. What contemporary woman have you observed who modeled Christlike behavior and taught you practical Christian truth by the way she lived her life?

   b. What specific things did you learn from her example?

7. Read John 3:1-18. What did you learn about how to witness effectively from the casual conversation Jesus had with Nicodemus?

8. Reread the story of Deborah Henry on pages 70-72.

   a. Describe what made her employer's daily treatment of her such a powerful evangelistic tool.

   b. Can you think of a time when a nonChristian recognized you as a believer? If so, what happened?

9. Read Matthew 5:12.

   a. Describe what you think the Bible means by "salt-seasoning."

   b. List some ways you can be "salt-seasoning" within your sphere of influence this week.

10. Look up the word "encourage" in the dictionary and write out the definition.

11. Read 1 Timothy 4:11-15. In this passage Paul is writing to his protégé, Timothy. Paul modeled excellence as a Christian mentor and gave important instruction and encouragement to Timothy as they

interacted with each other in person and by letter. As you read this passage, make a list of the important advice Paul gave to the young man he was mentoring.

12. Review the section in chapter 4 called "Practical Ways to Implement Jesus' Teaching" on pages 79-81.

   a. List the four action steps that will help us to follow through with Jesus' principle of influencing lives through our "walking and talking."

   b. How can you incorporate one of these ideas into your life this week? In the space below, write out what you think God wants you to do.

WEEK FIVE

Read chapter 5, "The Principle of Storytelling."

1. Read John 3:16-21. Write out why you think this passage has been referred to as "the greatest story ever told."

2. Good stories intrigue us and keep us listening. Stories are made up of a series of words that connect meaning to a plot or to an object lesson that keeps us guessing outcomes and responses. Words are the powerful vehicles that make stories possible.

    a. Memorize Proverbs 25:11.

    b. Paraphrase that verse in your own words below.

    c. Why do you think the Bible says well-chosen words are so important?

3. Review the story at the beginning of chapter 5.

    a. Describe the scriptural principle the story teaches.

    b. Read James 5:16 and Philippians 4:6-7. What specific points in these verses emphasize the main point of the story?

4. Read the section in chapter 5 called "Making Spiritual Truth Relevant" on pages 88-91. List everything you find in that section that helps us understand why people assimilate truth more easily through stories in today's culture.

5. Read Matthew 13:31-33 and Luke 13:8-10. Jesus often used ordinary objects to communicate spiritual truths. List any object lessons you find in these verses.

6. Mark 4:11 quotes Jesus telling the disciples: "You've been given insight into God's kingdom — you know how it works. But to those who can't see it yet, everything comes in stories, creating readiness, nudging them toward receptive insight." Review the story of Jay and

Melanie Stewart on pages 94-95.

   a. Describe how the skunk story nudged the Stewarts' neighbors toward "receptive insight."

   b. In your experience with nonChristians, do you think they would be more open to hearing the message of salvation presented within a story of what happened in someone else's life or by being confronted with the simple facts of the gospel? Explain.

7. Read the story Jesus told in Mark 4:1-20. What application did Jesus make clear to His disciples?

8. There is no more exciting story than the reality of a changed life. Read 2 Corinthians 5:17.

   a. Restate the verse in your own words.

   b. Describe what changes took place in your life when you became "a new creation in Christ."

9. Read the story of Jill Briscoe and Gabriela on pages 98-99. What was the most meaningful part of that story to you?

10. Read Deuteronomy 6:4-9.

   a. In your own words, describe what you believe Moses was asking people to do.

   b. How could telling the stories of Jesus help us to fulfill the commission in these verses?

11. Read the description of postmodernism that Lael Arrington depicts on page 100. Summarize the viewpoint many people have of life today.

12. Invite a younger Christian woman to have coffee or tea with you this week and ask her to share her story with you. If she is reluctant to do so on this visit, tell your own story of how you came to know that Jesus is "the greatest story ever told."

WEEK SIX

Read chapter 6, "The Principle of Asking Questions."

1. Memorize Mark 8:27-29. Write the verses on a card and review them each day this week.

2. Why do you think Jesus' question to Peter, "Who do you say I am?" was so important?

3. If Jesus asked you today, "Who do you say I am?" how would you respond?

4. One day Jesus encountered a blind beggar. The beggar recognized Jesus and must have instinctively known that this man could heal him. He said, "Jesus . . . have mercy on me!" (Luke 18:39). When Jesus asked that the man be brought to him, his first words were, "What do you want me to do for you?" (verse 41, NIV).

   a. Why do you think Jesus asked the man a question that seemed to have such an obvious answer?

   b. The man responded, "Lord, I want to see" (verse 41, NIV). Because God knows the longings of our hearts, do you think it is still important to verbalize our desires to Him? Why?

5. Carefully read Matthew 21:23-27.

   a. What was the question the chief priests and the elders asked Jesus?

   b. Why do you think Jesus didn't answer their question?

6. Review the story of Char, the teenager bent on a path of destruction, on pages 104-105. Why do you think a series of questions sometimes gets through to the heart of a person more effectively than a lecture?

7. Read Matthew 14:22-33.

    a. What was the key question Jesus asked Peter in this passage?

    b. How could Jesus' question have triggered growth in Peter's faith?

8. Jesus often asked questions to validate His teaching. One of the places He did was in the Sermon on the Mount. He said,

> *"Don't hoard treasure down here where it gets eaten by moths and corroded by rust or — worse! — stolen by burglars. Stockpile treasure in heaven, where it's safe from moth and rust and burglars. It's obvious, isn't it? The place where your treasure is, is the place you will most want to be, and end up being." (Matthew 6:19-21, emphasis added)*

    a. At what point in your life did this teaching "become obvious" to you? Describe what happened when you decided to invest your time, resources, and/or energy in God's work.

    b. For you, what is the most challenging part of "storing up treasure in heaven"?

9. One of the best ways to get to know a friend or someone you are mentoring is to ask good questions. During the next week, invite a younger woman (or a friend) over for coffee and ask the following questions from chapter 6. It might help you to be better prepared if you write out your own answers to these questions before you ask someone else to respond.

- What are your strengths? Your weaknesses?
- If you had a completely free day, what would you do?

- What are your hobbies, interests, and passions?
- If money were not an issue, what would you do with the rest of your life?
- What is the biggest roadblock between you and your dream?
- If you could interview any historical person, who would it be and what would you ask?
- In what two specific areas would you like to see yourself grow during the next one to three years?
- What is the biggest answer to prayer you've ever experienced?
- What is your favorite Scripture verse and why does it mean so much to you?
- What would you like to do for God in your lifetime?

Additional questions to ask a friend or a woman you are mentoring:

- How can I help you?
- How can I pray for you?

10. When Jesus was in terrible pain, dying on the cross, He asked the most gut-wrenching question of all time: "My God, my God, why have you forsaken me? Why are you so far from saving me, so far from the words of my groaning?" (Psalm 22:1, NIV). The obvious answer to that question is that He loves you and me. In the space below, write out your prayer of thanks to Him for being your personal Savior.

WEEK SEVEN

Read chapter 7, "The Principle of Compassion."

1. Memorize Matthew 25:35,40. Write out these verses and review them each day this week.

2. Look up the meaning of the word "compassion" in an English language dictionary or in a Bible dictionary. Then read the definition of compassion in the quotation by Megiddo Message at the beginning of the chapter. Compare both definitions and write out your own definition of this word in the space below.

3. Read Matthew 9:35-37. Part of this passage says, "When he looked out over the crowds, his heart broke."

   a. List some of the specific needs you see in the lives of the women in your immediate sphere of influence.

   b. On a scale of 1 to 10, how would you rate your "compassion quotient"?

   (Lowest)   *(Highest)*

   1   2   3   4   5   6   7   8   9   1 0

4. Review the story of Ruth Winslow's work in mainland China on pages 118-119. How does Ruth demonstrate "being Jesus" to the people she works with?

5. Review Matthew 14:13-14. This passage explains what Jesus did after He got the news that John the Baptist, His cousin and forerunner, had been beheaded.

   a. What was Jesus trying to do?

   b. How was He interrupted?

   c. What was His response?

6. Read the story in Mark 8:22-25. This story shows the role of compassionate friends in the life of a blind man. Can you recall a time in your own life when you needed spiritual or physical help and a compassionate person came alongside and met your need? If so, describe what took place.

7. Read the story of the healing that took place in Matthew 8:1-4. Then read Max Lucado's description of what it felt like to be a leper on pages 125-126 of this chapter.

   a. Why do you think Jesus demonstrated that having a compassionate heart often includes a healing touch?

   b. Describe why you think a touch can be so powerful when we are showing compassion to others.

8. Review Luke 15:11-31.

   a. List every phrase in this passage that shows compassion on the part of the father.

   b. How does this story demonstrate Jesus' model of compassion?

   c. How does the response of the older brother demonstrate the opposite of compassion?

9. Corrie ten Boom once said, "What have you done today that only a Christian would have done?"[4] Review the six bulleted points on page 129 that remind us of the steps involved in showing compassion. Write them out.

10. Meditate on Psalm 5:1-3, Psalm 51:12, Psalm 55:22, and Psalm 63:7-8. Write out your prayer of thanks to the Lord for His loving-kindness and compassion toward you.

WEEK EIGHT

Read chapter 8, "The Principle of Unconditional Love."

1. Memorize I Corinthians 13:4-7. Write out this passage on a card and rehearse it out loud every time you are alone this week.

2. What is your definition of unconditional love?

3. Read the story of the Samaritan woman in John 4:1-28.

   a. Describe what made this woman such an outcast.

   b. Make a list of things that cause women in today's culture to feel rejected and unloved.

4. Summarize the responses Jesus gives in the John 4 passage to the following paraphrases of the Samaritan woman's queries:

   • But I'm the wrong nationality.

   • How can you get living water when you don't even have a bucket?

   • I don't have a husband.

   • You're Jewish, so you think Jerusalem is the only place for worship, right?

5. What was the end result of the unconditional love Jesus displayed toward the Samaritan woman? (Review John 4:39-42.)

6. Read the paraphrase of I Corinthians 13:4-7 from Eugene Peterson's *The Message*, as it appears on pages 144-145. From that detailed description of love, list the five things that are the most important to you when receiving unconditional love from someone else.

7. Review the description of unconditional love John Powell describes on page 145.

a. What are the three important stages or moments in loving someone else according to Powell?

b. Read the first story in chapter 8 about J. P. and April. Have you
ever had trouble showing unconditional love? What has God
taught you?

8. Read Matthew 5:44-48. Summarize the instruction Jesus gives on
loving people who are unlovable.

9. Review John 3:16-18.

a. Based on these verses, how can an individual receive the unconditional love of God?

b. If you have already made this choice, explain what happened
when you received God's gift of love?

10. Look back at pages 153-154 and read the illustration Philip Yancey
wrote about his five-hour wait for a flight out of O'Hare Airport
one night.

a. If you were asked the same question the woman in the airport
asked Philip, "Do you ever just let God love you?" what would
your answer be? Explain.

b. Is there anything in your background or current experience that
keeps you from experiencing God's unconditional love? If so,
what will you do about it?

11. Read John 13:34-35; 14:15.

a. Write down what Jesus says we will do if we truly love Him.

b. Read Jeremiah 31:3 and write a responsive love letter to Jesus in
the form of a prayer.

Week Nine

Read chapter 9, "The Principle of Casting Vision."

1. Memorize Matthew 28:19.

    a. Write the verse on a card and refresh your memory by reading it daily.

    b. Paraphrase the verse in your own words.

2. Look up the word "vision" in a dictionary or in a Bible dictionary. Read the definition of vision given by Charles Swindoll at the beginning of chapter 9. Now paraphrase what you think it means "to cast vision" for someone else.

3. Jesus gave people a vision of what they could do with their potential. Read Matthew 16:17-19.

    a. How did Jesus describe the potential He saw in Peter?

    b. Read the story of Sherrie and her editor, Traci, on pages 163-165. How did Traci affirm the giftedness she saw in Sherrie?

4. Who was the first person outside of your family who made you feel you could do something great with your life? Describe how his or her validation and encouragement affected the vision you had of your worth and your future.

5. Review Matthew 10:39-42. Jesus prepared His followers for what to expect when they became His disciples. List five statements of advice and encouragement Jesus gave to those who followed Him:

6. Read Mark 16:15.

    a. Describe Jesus' instruction to His disciples in this verse.

    b. How do you think that mandate applies to you today?

7. Jesus gave basic survival instruction for Christians who want to fulfill

their mission and set an example for others. Read Matthew 5:11-16
and comment on His advice regarding the following topics:

  a. Receiving negative criticism

  b. Being salt-seasoning

  c. Illuminating the world

8. When we move forward and accept the challenging, visionary task
God has for us, He gives us great encouragement through His Word.
Write a summary of the following verses:

  a. Psalm 32:8

  b. Psalm 34:4

  c. Jeremiah 29:11-13

  d. Micah 6:8

9. Review the section in chapter 9 on visionary people of influence, pages
169-173. Next to their names, write a phrase that describes the type of
encouragement they gave to the women they mentored.

  a. Miss Harvey

  b. Jayne's "back row ladies"

  c. Mr. Farinella

  d. Dr. Paula Martinez

10. When we stay with what is "safe," we may never risk the joy, the
challenge, the friendship, the fulfillment, and the exhilaration of
intentionally impacting lives as Jesus did.

  a. Read the instructions Paul gave to his mentee, Timothy, in 2
Timothy 2:2.

  b. What is the main point Paul is making in this verse?

11. Review and memorize Matthew 28:19. Write a statement describing what you believe God is asking you to do to fulfill His vision for
your future.

12. Write out your prayer of response to God or use the following
    example:

> *Lord, I'm available. Reveal Your vision to me. I am no*
> *longer content to live a safe Christian life. Move me out*
> *of my comfort zone. I long for an adventure in trusting*
> *You. I hang my weakness on Your strength. I want to live*
> *out the principles Jesus modeled. I want to be a woman*
> *of influence who is making a lasting impact on others.*
> *Amen.*

NOTES

CHAPTER ONE: IMPACTING LIVES LIKE JESUS DID

1. Donna Otto, "Discover the Mentor in You," *Virtue,* July/August 1996, p. 39.
2. J. Oswald Sanders, *Spiritual Leadership* (Chicago: Moody, 1967), p. 40.

CHAPTER TWO: LEARNING FROM THE MASTER

1. Lori Salierno, *The Exclamation,* Fall, 1997, p. 6.
2. Elisabeth Elliot, quoted from a message delivered at Women's Day Away, Minneapolis, September 1976.
3. Esther Burroughs, as quoted by Mary Cagney in "Mentoring and Modeling Great Aspirations," *Christianity Today*, April 6, 1998, p. 56.
4. Laurie Beth Jones, *Jesus CEO* (New York: Hyperion Press, 1992), pp. xiii-xiv.
5. Becky Tirabassi, "The Blessings and Benefits of Prayer," as quoted by Judith Couchman in *One Holy Passion* (Colorado Springs, CO: WaterBrook Press, 1998), p. 200.
6. Tirabassi, p. 201.
7. *NetFax*, Leadership Network, August 1998, p. 1.
8. Bill Gove, quoted in "Speaking Tip #2," from his videotape *Everything You Need to Know About Speaking*, March 16, 1998, p. 1.
9. Gove, p. 1.
10. Bobb Biehl, *Mentoring* (Nashville, TN: Broadman & Holman, 1996), p. 42.
11. Summarized from several Bible dictionaries.

12. Saint Exupery, as quoted in *The International Thesaurus of Quotations* (New York: Harper & Row, 1970), p. 473.

13. Marilyn Meberg, *I'd Rather Be Laughing* (Nashville, TN: Word, 1998), p. 157.

14. Bill Hybels, as quoted in *NetFax*, Leadership Network, No. 100, June 22, 1998.

CHAPTER THREE: THE PRINCIPLE OF TIME ALONE WITH GOD

1. Becky Tirabassi, as quoted in *Closer to God* (Wheaton, IL: Tyndale, 1996), p. 96.

2. Richard Foster, *Celebration of Discipline* (San Francisco: Harper & Row, 1978), pp. 84-85.

3. Wesley Duewel, *Touch the World Through Prayer* (Grand Rapids, MI: Zondervan, 1986), pp. 96-97.

4. Charles Swindoll, in the foreword to Paul Cedar, *A Life of Prayer* (Nashville, TN: Word, 1998), p. ix.

5. Taken from *Fresh Wind, Fresh Fire*, by Jim Cymbala with Dean Merrill. Copyright © 1997 by Jim Cymbala. Used by permission of Zondervan Publishing House.

6. Cymbala, p. 27.

7. Horatio G. Spafford, Public Domain.

8. Philip Yancey, *The Jesus I Never Knew* (Grand Rapids, MI: Zondervan, 1995), p. 265.

9. Marlee Alex, "The Sound of His Voice," *Virtue*, September/October 1991, p. 4.

CHAPTER FOUR: THE PRINCIPLE OF WALKING AND TALKING

1. Marilyn Quayle, as quoted in *Closer to God* (Wheaton, IL: Tyndale, 1996), pp. 38, 56.

2. Esther Burroughs, as quoted by Mary Cagney in "Mentoring and Modeling Great Aspirations," *Christianity Today*, April 6, 1998, p. 55.

3. Susan Hunt, *Spiritual Mothering* (Wheaton, IL: Crossway, 1992), pp. 3-4.

4. Kathy Peel, as quoted in *Closer to God* (Wheaton, IL: Tyndale, 1996), p. 66.

5. Pam Farrel, *Woman of Influence* (Downers Grove, IL: InterVarsity, 1996), pp. 158-169.

CHAPTER FIVE: THE PRINCIPLE OF STORYTELLING

1. Max McLean, "Fellowship for the Performing Arts" newsletter, October 21, 1998.
2. Max McLean, Leadership Network, *NetFax*, No. 102, July 20, 1998.
3. George Barna, *The Second Coming of the Church* (Nashville, TN: Word Publishing 1998), p. 71.
4. Jim Lyon, "Building Bridges to the World," *People to People*, September 1997, vol. 18, no. 9, p. 2.
5. Lyon, p. 2.
6. Barna, p. 72
7. Jill Briscoe, "Telling the Truth" newsletter, July 1998, pp. 1-2.
8. Lael Arrington, quoted from a lecture titled "Thoroughly Postmodern Millie and Willie," delivered at the Advanced Speak Up With Confidence seminar, Hillsdale, MI, July 24, 1998.

CHAPTER SIX: THE PRINCIPLE OF ASKING QUESTIONS

1. Candy Davison, quoted in a message titled, "What's Your Problem?" at Sandy Cove Conference Center, North East, MD, in January, 1999.
2. Robert C. Crosby and Pamela Crosby, "Now That's a Good Question," *Focus on the Family*, December 1996, p. 7.
3. Karen Lee-Thorp, *How to Ask Great Questions* (Colorado Springs, CO: NavPress, 1998), p. 5.
4. Bobb Biehl, *Mentoring* (Nashville, TN: Broadman & Holman, 1996), p. 42.
5. Todd Catteau, "The Questions of Jesus," *Discipleship Journal*, No. 10, July/August 1997, p. 24.
6. Hebrews 13:5, NIV.
7. Tom McNichol, "Who Was Jesus?" *USA Weekend*, December 18-20, 1992, pp. 4-5.
8. Leola Floren, used by permission.

CHAPTER SEVEN: THE PRINCIPLE OF COMPASSION

1. Megiddo Message, as quoted by Lloyd Cory, *Quotable Quotations* (Wheaton, IL: Victor, 1985), p. 76.
2. Spiros Zodhiates, Th.D., *The Complete Word Study Dictionary* (Chattanooga, TN: AMG Publishers, 1992), p. 1306.
3. From *Keep Me Faithful,* by Ruth Harms Calkin, copyright © 1996. Used by permission of Tyndale House Publishers, Inc. All rights reserved.
4. Max Lucado, *Just Like Jesus* (Nashville, TN: Word, 1998), pp. 29-30.
5. Lucado, p. 30.
6. Corrie ten Boom, *Clippings from My Notebook* (Minneapolis: World Wide, 1982), p. 115.
7. Jess Moody, as quoted by Cory, p. 76.
8. Author unknown, as quoted by Albert M. Wells, Jr., in *Inspiring Quotations* (Nashville, TN: Thomas Nelson, 1988), p. 47.
9. Author unknown, reprinted from "Wednesday Wisdom for Living Well," by Janice Krouskop, November 11, 1998.

CHAPTER EIGHT: THE PRINCIPLE OF UNCONDITIONAL LOVE

1. John Powell, *Unconditional Love* (Niles, IL: Argus Communications, 1978), p. 68.
2. For an update on April and J.P., see *When I Lay My Isaac Down* (NavPress, 2004). A DVD teaching series is also available.
3. *The Quest Study Bible* (Grand Rapids, MI: Zondervan, 1994), p. 1471.
4. Augustine, as quoted by Lloyd Cory, *Quotable Quotations* (Wheaton, IL: Victor, 1985), p. 211.
5. Powell, p. 109.
6. Powell, pp. 83-84.
7. Billy Graham as quoted by Lloyd Cory, *Quotable Quotations* (Wheaton, IL: Victor, 1985), p. 226.
8. Philip Yancey, *The Jesus I Never Knew* (Grand Rapids, MI: Zondervan, 1995), p. 269.

Chapter Nine: The Principle of Casting Vision

1. Charles Swindoll, *The Tale of the Tardy Oxcart* (Nashville, TN: Word Publishing, 1998), p. 606.
2. Quote contributed by Carol John from a Bible study lecture by Margaret Frost.
3. Bill Hybels, "Lead, Manage, Shepherd, Teach," from the "Defining Moments, Legacy of a Leader" tape series.
4. Hybels, 43, pp. 1-2.
5. Bobb Biehl, *Mentoring* (Nashville, TN: Broadman & Holman, 1996), p. 179.
6. Henrietta Mears, as quoted by Earl O. Roe in *Dream Big: The Henrietta Mears Story* (Ventura, CA: Regal, 1990), pp. 17-18.
7. Jan Johnson, "What If I Fail?" *Virtue Magazine*, May/June 1994, p. 46.
8. Os Guinness, *The Call* (Nashville, TN: Word, 1998), p. 7.

Nine-Week Bible Study

1. Elisabeth Elliot, *Keep a Quiet Heart* (Ann Arbor, MI: Servant, 1995), p. 11.
2. Linda Dillow, *Calm My Anxious Heart* (Colorado Springs, CO: NavPress, 1998), p. 197.
3. J. Oswald Sanders, *Spiritual Leadership* (Chicago: Moody, 1967), p. 40.
4. Corrie ten Boom, *Clippings from My Notebook* (Minneapolis, MN: World Wide, 1982), p. 115.

ABOUT THE AUTHOR

CAROL KENT is a popular international public speaker best known for being dynamic, humorous, encouraging, and biblical. A favorite on many radio and television programs, Carol enjoys sharing the life lessons from her best-selling books, which include: *When I Lay My Isaac Down*, *Becoming a Woman of Influence*, *Mothers Have Angel Wings*, *Secret Longings of the Heart*, *Tame Your Fears*, *Speak Up With Confidence*, and *Detours, Tow Trucks, and Angels in Disguise* (all NavPress). She has also cowritten with Karen Lee-Thorp the DESIGNED FOR INFLUENCE Bible Studies (six books in the series, NavPress). Carol was also the coauthor and general editor of the KISSES OF SUNSHINE Series of five books (Zondervan). She has been featured on the cover of *Today's Christian Woman* and her articles have been published in a wide variety of magazines. Carol has spoken internationally in Germany, Bulgaria, China, Korea, Hong Kong, Guatemala, Mexico, and Canada.

She has recently entered the public eye with the story of her only son's imprisonment for murder, a journey she shared in the powerful book *When I Lay My Isaac Down*. This painful experience has led Carol and her husband, Gene, down a long road of sacrifice and redemption, allowing her to better understand what a "woman of influence" truly is.

She is the president of Speak Up Speaker Services, a Christian speakers' bureau, and the founder and director of Speak Up With Confidence seminars, a ministry committed to helping Christians develop their communication skills. She has recently founded the nonprofit organization, Speak Up for Hope, providing encouragement to families of incarcerated individuals. She holds a master's degree in communication arts and a bachelor's degree in speech education.

For information on scheduling Carol to speak, contact:

SPEAK UP SPEAKER SERVICES
Call toll-free: (888) 870-7719
www.CarolKent.org
www.SpeakUpSpeakerServices.com

OTHER LIFE-CHANGING BOOKS BY CAROL KENT.

When I Lay My Isaac Down
1-57683-474-3
For the first time, best-selling author Carol Kent shares the heartbreaking story of her son, Jason, with the world. Her moving testimony to God's faithfulness will alter the way you think about personal challenges.

When I Lay My Isaac Down DVD
1-57683-958-3
This interactive companion to the best-selling *When I Lay My Isaac Down* comes with everything you need for facilitating more than two months of life-changing small-group discussion or a one-day women's retreat.

Tame Your Fears
1-57683-359-3
If you've grown tired of being victimized by fear, let Carol Kent show you how to tame your fears and move toward a more productive and satisfying future.

Secret Longings of the Heart
1-57683-360-7
Here is a rich encounter with the hidden desires of women today—the passions that determine lifestyle, behavior, and attitudes—and how these relate to serving and loving God.